1972

ertime.

RUPERT BROOKE

RUPERT BROOKE

RUPERT BROOKE AND THE
INTELLECTUAL IMAGINATION

by

Walter de la Mare

—

RECOLLECTIONS OF RUPERT BROOKE

by

Maurice Browne

—

DEMOCRACY AND THE ARTS

by

Rupert Brooke

With a Preface by Geoffrey Keynes

KENNIKAT PRESS/Port Washington, N.Y. 11050

RUPERT BROOKE

Rupert Brooke and the Intellectual Imagination
by Walter de la Mare first published 1919

Recollections of Rupert Brooke
by Maurice Browne first published 1927

Democracy and the Arts
by Rupert Brooke first published 1946

Reissued as Three Volumes in One by Kennikat Press in 1968

Library of Congress Catalog Card No: 68-8248
Manufactured in the United States of America

Rupert Brooke and the Intellectual Imagination

A Lecture
by
Walter de la Mare

Rupert Brooke and the Intellectual Imagination

ONE evening in 1766, Dr Johnson being then in the fifty-seventh year of his age, his friends, Boswell and Goldsmith, called on him at his lodgings in Johnson's Court, Fleet Street, with the intention of persuading him to sup with them at the Mitre. But though he was proof against their cajoleries, he was by no means averse from a talk. With true hospitality, since he had himself, we are told, become a water-drinker, he called for a bottle of port. This his guests proceeded to discuss. While they sipped, the three of them conversed on subjects no less beguiling than playgoing and poetry.

Goldsmith ventured to refer to the deplorable fact that his old friend and former schoolfellow had given up the writing of verses. "Why, sir," replied Johnson, " our tastes greatly alter. The lad does not care for the child's rattle. . . . As we advance in the journey of life, we drop some of the things which have pleased us ; whether it be that we are fatigued and don't choose to carry so many things any farther, or that we find other things which we like better."

Boswell persisted. "But, sir," said he, "why don't you give us something in some other way." "No, sir," Johnson replied, "I am not obliged to do any more. No man is obliged to do as much as he can do. A man is to have part of his life to himself." "But I wonder, sir," Boswell continued, "you have not more pleasure in writing than in not writing." Whereupon descended the crushing retort, "Sir, you *may* wonder."

Johnson then proceeded to discuss the actual making of verses. "The great difficulty," he observed—alas, how truly, "is to know when you have made good ones." Once, he boasted, he had written as many as a full hundred lines a day; but he was then under forty, and had been inspired by no less fertile a theme than "The Vanity of Human Wishes," a poem that, with other prudent counsel, bids the "young enthusiast" pause ere he choose literature and learning as a spiral staircase to fame :—

> Deign on the passing world to turn thine eyes
> And pause awhile from Letters, to be wise . . .

None the less, Johnson made haste to assure Goldsmith that his Muse even at this late day was not wholly mum :—"I am not quite idle; I made one line t'other day; but I made no more."

"Let us hear it," cried Goldsmith, "we'll put a bad one to it!" "No, sir, I have forgot it." And so sally succeeded sally.

How much of the virtue of Johnson's talk we are to attribute to Boswell's genius for selection and condensation, and how much to the habituality of his idol's supreme judgment, penetration, humanity and good sense, is one of the delectable problems of literature. This fact, at any rate, is unquestionable; namely, that Johnson seldom indeed let fall a remark, even though merely in passing, which is not worth a sensible man's consideration. He knew—rare felicity—what he was talking about. He spoke—rare presence of mind—not without, but after, aforethought. However dogmatic, overbearing and partisan he might be, not only in what he is recorded to have said is there always something substantive and four-square, but frequently even a light and occasional utterance of his will stand like a signpost at the cross-roads positively imploring the traveller to make further exploration.

"The lad does not care for the child's rattle." Here, surely, is one of those signposts, one more enticing invitation to explore. By rattle, obviously, Johnson meant not only things childish, but things childlike. For such things the 'lad' does not merely cease to care. He substitutes for them other things which he likes better. Not that every vestige of charm and sentiment necessarily deserts the rattle, but other delights intrude ; and, what is still more important, other faculties that will take pleasure in these new toys and interests come into energy and play. Does not this rightly imply that between childhood and boyhood is fixed a perceptible gulf, physical, spiritual, psychological, and that in minds in which the powers and tendencies conspicuous in boyhood, and more or less dormant or latent in earlier years, predominate, those of childhood are apt to fade and fall away ?

This is true, I think, of us all, whatever our gifts and graces ; but in a certain direction I believe it is true in a peculiar degree of poets— of children and lads (and possibly lasses, though they, fortunately for me, lie outside my immediate inquiry) who are destined, or doomed, to become poets. Poets, that is, may be divided, for illustration and convenience, into two distinct classes : those who in their idiosyncrasies resemble children and bring to ripeness the faculties peculiar to childhood ; and those who resemble lads. On the one hand is the poet who carries with him through life, in varying vigour and variety, the salient characteristics of childhood (though modified, of course, by subsequent

activities and experience). On the other is the
poet who carries with him the salient characteristics of boyhood (though modified by the experiences and activities of his childhood). This
is little more than a theory, but it may be worth
a passing scrutiny.

What are the salient characteristics of childhood ? Children, it will be agreed, live in a
world peculiarly their own, so much so that it
is doubtful if the adult can do more than very
fleetingly reoccupy that far-away consciousness.
There is, however, no doubt that the world of
the grown-up is to children an inexhaustible
astonishment and despair. They brood on us.
And perhaps it is well that we are not invited
to their pow-wows, until, at any rate, the hatchet
for the hundredth time is re-buried. Children
are in a sense butterflies, though they toil with
an almost inconceivable assiduity after life's
scanty pollen and nectar, and though, by a curious
inversion of the processes of nature, they may become the half-comatose and purblind chrysalides
which too many of us poor mature creatures so
ruefully resemble. They are not bound in by
their groping senses. Facts to them are the live-
liest of chameleons. Between their dream and
their reality looms no impassable abyss. There
is no solitude more secluded than a child's, no

absorption more complete, no insight more exquisite and, one might even add, more compre-
hensive. As we strive to look back and to
live our past again, can we recall any joy, fear,
hope or disappointment more extreme than those
of our childhood, any love more impulsive and
unquestioning, and, alas, any boredom so un-
mitigated and unutterable ?

We call their faith, even in ourselves, credulity ;
and are grown perhaps so accustomed to life's
mysteries that we pale at their candour. " I am
afraid you cannot understand it, dear," exclaimed a long-suffering mother, at the end of her
resources. " O yes, I can very well," was her
little boy's reply, " if only you would not ex-
plain." " Why is there such a lot of things in
the world if no one knows all these things ? "
ran another small mind's inquiry. And yet
another : " Perhaps the world is a fancy, mother.
Shall I wake from this dream ? "

We speak indulgently of childish make-believe,
childish fancy. Bret Harte was nearer the truth
when he maintained that " the dominant expression of a child is gravity." The cold fact
is that few of us have the energy to be serious at
their pitch. There runs a jingle :

> O, whither go all the nights and days ?
> And where can to-morrow be ?

> Is anyone there, when *I*'m not there ?
> And why am I always Me ?

With such metaphysical riddles as these—riddles which no philosopher has yet answered to anybody's but his own entire satisfaction —children entertain the waking moments of their inward reverie. They are contemplatives, solitaries, fakirs, who sink again and again out of the noise and fever of existence into a waking vision. We can approach them only by way of intuition and remembrance, only by becoming even as one of them ; though there are many books—Sully's " Studies of Childhood," for instance, Mr Gosse's " Father and Son," John Ruskin's " Præterita," Serge Aksakoff's " Years of Childhood," Henry James's " A Small Boy and Others "—which will be a really vivid and quiet help in times of difficulty.

This broken dream, then, this profound self-communion, this innocent peace and wonder make up the secret existence of a really child-like child : while the intellect is only stirring.

Then, suddenly life flings open the door of the nursery. The child becomes a boy. I do not mean that the transformation is as instantaneous as that, though, if I may venture to give a personal testimony, I have seen two children plunge out into the morning for the first time to their first boys'-school, and return at evening transmogrified, so to speak, into that queer, wild, and (frequently) amiable animal known as a boy. Gradually the childish self retires like a shocked snail into its shell. Like a hermit crab it accumulates defensive and aggressive disguises. Consciousness from being chiefly subjective becomes largely objective. The steam-engine routs Faërie. Actuality breaks in upon dream. School rounds off the glistening angles. The individual is swamped awhile by the collective. Yet the child-mind, the child-imagination persists, and if powerful, never perishes.

But *here*, as it seems to me, is the dividing line. It is here that the boyish type of mind and imagination, the intellectual analytical type begins to show itself, and to flourish. The boy—I merely refer, if I may be forgiven, to Boy, and far more tentatively to Girl, in the abstract, though, of course, there is no such entity—the boy is happy in company. Company sharpens his wits, awakens his rivalry, deepens his responsiveness, enlarges his responsibility, " stirs him up," as we say. Apron-strings, however dear their contents, were always a little restrictive. He borrows a pitiless pair of scissors. He, unlike the child told of by Blake and Vaughan and Traherne, had always more or less " under-

stood this place." He loves " a forward motion "
—the faster the better. When " shades of the
prison-house " begin to close about him, he immediately sets out to explore the jail. His
natural impulse is to discover the thronging,
complicated, busy world, to sail out into the
West, rather than to dream of a remote Orient.
He is a restless, curious, untiring inquirer;
though preferably on his own lines rather than
on those dictated to him. He wants to test, to
examine, to experiment.

We must beware of theories and pigeon-holes.
Theory is a bad master, and there is a secret
exit to every convenient pigeon-hole. There are
children desperately matter-of-fact; there are
boys dreamily matter-of-fancy. But roughly,
these are the two phases of man's early life.
Surroundings and education may mould and
modify, but the inward bent of each one of
us is persistent. Can we not, indeed, divide
"grown-ups" into two distinct categories;
those in whom the child is most evident, and
those resembling the boy? "Men are but children
of a larger growth," says Dryden. And Praed
makes fun of the sad fact: "Bearded men today appear just Eton boys grown heavy." The
change is one of size rather than one of quality.
Indeed, in its fight for a place, in its fair play

and foul, in its rigid conventions, in its contest for prizes that are so oddly apt to lose their value as soon as they are won, how like the school of life is to any other school ; how strangely opinions differ regarding its rules, its aims, its method, its routine and its Headmaster.

And the poets ? They, too, attend both schools. But what are the faculties and qualities of mind which produce poetry, or which incline men towards it ? According to Byron, there are four elements that we are justified in demanding of a poet. He found them, not without satisfaction, more conspicuous in Pope than in his contemporaries. These elements are sense, learning (in moderation), passion and invention. Perhaps because he was less rich in it, he omitted a fifth element, by no means the least essential. I mean imagination, the imagination that not merely invents, but that creates, and pierces to the inmost spirit and being of life, humanity and nature. This poetical imagination also is of two distinct kinds or types. The one divines, the other discovers. The one is intuitive, inductive ; the other logical, deductive. The one visionary, the other intellectual. The one knows that beauty is truth, the other proves that truth is beauty. And the poet inherits, as it seems to me, the one kind from the child in him, the other from the boy in him. Not that any one poet's imagination is purely and solely of either type. The greatest poets—Shakespeare, Dante, Goëthe, for instance, are masters of both. Other poets, Wordsworth, Keats, Patmore, for instance, may manifest in varying measure the one impulse and the other. But the two streams, though their source and tributaries intermingle, are distinguishable; and such poets as Plato, the writer of the Book of Job, Vaughan, Blake, Coleridge, and Shelley, may be taken as representative of the one type; Lucretius, Donne, Dryden, Byron, Browning, Meredith, as representative of the other. Is not life both a dream and an awakening?

The visionaries, those whose eyes are fixed on the distance, on the beginning and end, rather than on the incident and excitement, of life's journey, have to learn to substantiate their imaginings, to base their fantastic palaces on *terra firma,* to weave their dreams into the fabric of actuality. But the source and origin of their poetry is in the world within. The intellectual imagination, on the other hand, flourishes on knowledge and experience. It must first explore before it can analyse, devour before it can digest, the world in which it finds itself. It feeds and feeds upon ideas, but because it is creative, it expresses them in the terms of

humanity, of the senses and the emotions, makes
life of them, that is. There is less mystery, less
magic in its poetry. It does not demand of its
reader so profound or so complete a surrender.
But if any youthfulness is left in us, we can share
its courage, enthusiasm and energy, its zest and
enterprise, its penetrating thought, its wit,
fervour, passion, and we should not find it
impossible to sympathise with its wild revulsions
of faith and feeling, its creative scepticism.

Without imagination of the one kind or the
other mortal existence is indeed a dreary and
prosaic business. The moment we begin to *live*
—when we meet the friend of friends, or fall in
love, or think of our children, or make up our
minds, or set to the work we burn to do, or make
something, or vow a vow, or pause suddenly face
to face with beauty—at that moment the imagination in us kindles, begins to flame. Then
we actually talk in rhythm. What is genius
but the possession of this supreme inward energy
in a rare and intense degree ? Illumined by the
imagination, our life—whatever its defeats and
despairs—is a never-ending, unforeseen strangeness and adventure and mystery. This is the
fountain of our faith and of our hope.

And so, by what I am afraid has been a tediously
circuitous route, I have come at length to

Rupert Brooke and to *his* poetry. His surely was the intellectual imagination possessed in a rare degree. Nothing in his work is more conspicuous than its preoccupation with actual experience, its adventurousness, its daring, its keen curiosity and interest in ideas, its life-giving youthfulness. Nothing in his work is more conspicuous by its absence than reverie, a deep still broodingness. The children in his poems are few. They are all seen objectively, from without; though a wistful childlike longing for peace and home and mother dwells in such a poem as " Retrospect " or " A Memory." I am not sure that the word ' dream ' occurs in them at all.*

" Don't give away one of the first poets in England," he says in one of his letters, " but there is in him still a very, very small portion that's just a little childish." Surely it was the *boy* in him that boasted in that jolly, easy fashion, the boy in him that was a little shamefaced to confess to that faint vestige of childishness.

* To my shame and consternation my friend Mr Edward Marsh has pointed out to me, since this paper was read, that the word ' dream ' occurs in no less than fifteen of Brooke's poems. This, I hope, will be one more salutary lesson that general impressions are none the worse for being put to a close test. Still, the fact that that peculiar, dreamlike quality and atmosphere which is so conspicuous in the poetry of the visionaries is very rarely, if ever, present in that of Brooke will not, I think, be gainsaid.

The theme of his poetry is the life of the mind, the senses, the feelings, life here and now, however impatient he may be with life's limitations. Its longing is for a state of consciousness wherein this kind of life shall be possible without exhaustion, disillusionment, or reaction. His words, too, are not symbols ; they mean precisely what they say and only what they say. Whereas the words of the mystics of the childlike imagination, Blake and Vaughan and Coleridge, seem chiefly to mean what is left hinted at, rather than expressed. His world stands out sharp and distinct, like the towers and pinnacles of a city under the light and blue of the sky. Their world, old as Eden and remote as the stars, lies like the fabric of a vision, bathed in an unearthly atmosphere. He desired, loved, and praised things in themselves for their energy, vividness and naturalness ; they for some inward and spiritual significance, for the reality of which they are the painted veil. *They* live in the quietude of their imaginations, in a far-away listening, and are most happy when at peace, if not passive. He is all activity, apprehensiveness.

Nothing pleases him so much as doing things, though, fretted that body and mind so soon weary, he may pine for sleep. His writing, whether in his poems, his " Webster," or in his letters, is itself a kind of action ; and he delights far more than the mystics in things touched, smelt and tasted. He delights, that is, in things in themselves not merely for their beauty or for the unseen reality they represent. He is restless, enquiring, veers in the wind like a golden weathercock. He is impatient of a vague idealism, as wary as a fox of the faintest sniff of sentimentality. To avoid them (not always quite successfully,) he flies to the opposite extreme, and to escape from what he calls the rosy mists of poets' experience emphasises the unpleasant side of life. His one desire is to tell each salient moment's truth about it. Truth at all costs : let beauty take care of itself. So he came to write and to defend poems that in Mr Marsh's witty phrase one finds it disquieting to read at meals. A child, a visionary, lives in eternity ; a man in time, a boy—sheer youthfulness—in the moment. It is the moments that flower for Brooke. What is his poem " Dining-room Tea " but the lovely cage of an instant when in ecstasy time and the world stood still ?

For truth's sake he has no fear of contradictions. The mood changes, the problem, even the certainty shows itself under different aspects ; he will be faithful to each in turn. Obviously he rather enjoyed shocking the stagnant and satisfied, and baiting the thin-blooded philosophers, enjoyed indeed shocking and baiting himself; but he also delighted, for the pure intellectual exercise, in looking, as we say, all round a thing. If, unlike Methuselah, he did not live long enough to see life whole, he at least confronted it with a remarkably steady and disconcerting stare. If he was anywhere at ease, it was in " the little nowhere of the brain." Again and again, for instance, he speculates on the life that follows death. First (mere chronological order is not absolutely material) he imagines the Heaven of the fish:

> Fat caterpillars drift around,
> And Paradisal grubs are found;
> Unfading moths, immortal flies,
> And the worm that never dies.
> And in that Heaven of all their wish,
> There shall be no more land, say fish.

Next, he laments despairingly in Tahiti, with a kind of wistful mockery, at the thought of an immortality wherein all is typical and nothing real:

> And you'll no longer swing and sway
> Divinely down the scented shade,
> Where feet to Ambulation fade,
> And moons are lost in endless Day.
> How shall we wind these wreaths of ours,
> Where there are neither heads nor flowers? . . .

Next, he momentarily wafts himself into the being of a Shade :

> So a poor ghost, beside his misty streams,
> Is haunted by strange doubts, evasive dreams,
>   Hints of a pre-Lethean life, of men,
> Stars, rocks, and flesh, things unintelligible,
>   And light on waving grass, he knows not when,
> And feet that ran, but where, he cannot tell.

Next, he deprecates the possibility of a future life even as tenuous and nebulous as this :

> Poor straws ! on the dark flood we catch awhile,
>   Cling, and are borne into the night apart.
>   The laugh dies with the lips, 'Love' with the lover.

And, again, he is lost in rapture at the possibility which he mocked at in the first poem, sighed at in the second, belittled in the third, and denied in the fourth :

> Not dead, not undesirous yet,
>   Still sentient, still unsatisfied,
> We'll ride the air, and shine, and flit,
>   Around the places where we died,
>
> And dance as dust before the sun,
>   And light of foot, and unconfined,
> Hurry from road to road, and run
>   About the errands of the wind.

And every mote, on earth or air,
  Will speed and gleam, down later days,
And like a secret pilgrim fare
  By eager and invisible ways,

Nor ever rest, nor ever lie,
  Till, beyond thinking, out of view,
One mote of all the dust that's I
  Shall meet one atom that was you.

Then in some garden hushed from wind,
  Warm in a sunset's afterglow,
The lovers in the flowers will find
  A sweet and strange unquiet grow

Upon the peace ; and, past desiring,
  So high a beauty in the air,
And such a light, and such a quiring,
  And such a radiant ecstasy there,

They'll know not if it's fire, or dew,
  Or out of earth, or in the height,
Singing, or flame, or scent, or hue,
  Or two that pass, in light, to light,

Out of the garden, higher, higher. . . .

Which of these conflicting solutions, we may
inquire, to one of Life's obscurest problems are we
to accept as his ?   Do, or do not, such seductive
speculations as these confirm the view expressed
by Plato in the *Republic* that the poets
undermine the rational principle in the soul ?
It may be admitted that such poetry as this, in

the words of Bacon, " makes men witty," and is
unquestionably a " criticism of life "; but can it
be said to teach—as Wordsworth intended that
his poetry should ? Well, when Mrs Barbauld
had the temerity to charge " The Rime of the
Ancient Mariner " with two grave faults ; first,
that it was improbable, and next, that it had no
moral ; Coleridge cheerfully pleaded guilty to the
first charge, while, as for the other, " I told her
that . . . it had too much—that is, for a work
of pure imagination." Will it satisfy " serious "
inquirers if it be suggested that these poems of
Brooke's are manifestations of the intellectual
imagination ? Probably not. They demand of
a poet a definite and explicit philosophy. They
desire of him a confirmation, if not of their own
faith, then of his. But it cannot be too clearly
recognised that the faith of a poet is expressed in
all that he writes. He cannot, either as a man
or as a poet, live without faith ; and never does.
A few lovely words about lovely things is an
expression of faith : so, too, is all love, all desire
for truth, all happiness. If we have such faith
ourselves, if we search close enough, we shall
find a poet's faith expressed implicitly throughout his work.

We must, too, be thankful for many and various
mercies, the mercy, for instance (so richly con-

ferred in Brooke's writing) that here was a man
who never spared mind and spirit in the effort
to do the best work he could, who was that
finest thing any man can be—a true craftsman
delighting in his job. We cannot demand that a
poet shall answer each of our riddles in turn ;
" tidy things up." He shares our doubts and
problems ; exults in them, and at the same time
proves that life in spite of all its duplicity and
deceits and horrors, is full of strangeness, wonder,
mystery, grace and power : is " good." This,
at any rate, is true of Rupert Brooke. And he
knew well enough that the nearer a poet gets to
preaching, the more cautious he should be re-
specting the pulpit and the appurtenances thereof.

As with the life hereafter, so with this life, so
with love. The sentimentalist always shy of the
real, the cynic always hostile to it, cling to some
pleasing dream or ugly nightmare of the real,
knowing them to be illusions. That is precisely
what Brooke, keen, insistent, analytical, refused
to do. He pours out his mind and heart for
instance in the service of love. The instant
that love is dead, he has, to put it crudely, very
little use for its corpse. He refuses point blank
to find happiness in any happy medium, to be a
wanderer, as he said, in " the middle mist."
There are two sides—many more than two, as a

matter of fact—to every question. "Blue Evening" or "The Voice" prove his competence to see both. At times, indeed, with a kind of boyish waywardness and obstinacy he prefers the other side—the ugliest—of the much-flattered moon. Helen's young face was beautiful. True. In age not only must she have lost her now immortal fairness, but possibly she became repulsive. Well, then, as a poet, hating "sugared lies," he said so.

It is indeed characteristic of the intellectual imagination to insist on 'life's little ironies.' It destroys in order to rebuild. Every scientist, who is not a mere accumulator of facts, possesses it. Acutely sensitive to the imperfections of the present, its hope is in the future ; whereas the visionary, certainly no less conscious of flaw and evil, is happy in his faith in the past, or rather in the eternal now. The one cries " What shall I do ? " the other "What must I be ? " The one, as has been said, would prove that truth is beauty ; the other knows that beauty is truth. After all, to gain the *whole* world is in one true sense to save the soul.

In the lugubrious and exciting moment when Brooke wrote " Kindliness " and " Menelaus and Helen," it was not his aim or thought to see that age, no less than youth and beauty is, in his own

phrase, ' pitiful with mortality.' He resented
ugliness and decay, and associated them with
death and evil. For death, whatever else it
may be, brings destruction of the beauty of the
body; and evil brings the destruction of the spirit
which is the life and light of the body. They
are the contraries of a true living energy ; and
because his mind seemed to be indestructible,
and his body as quick with vitality as a racehorse,
and love the very lantern of beauty, he not only
feared the activities of death, but was intolerant
of mere tranquillity, even of friendliness, and,
above all, of masking make-believe.

Sometimes, indeed, in his poetry, in his letters,
he is not quite just to himself in the past, or
even in the present, because he seemed to detect
compromise and pretence. " So the poor love
of fool and blind I've proved you, For, fool or
lovely, 'twas a fool that loved you." On the
other hand, listen to these fragments from the
letters in Mr Marsh's vivifying memoir, " I find
myself smiling a dim, gentle, poetic, paternal
Jehovah-like smile—over the ultimate excellence of humanity." " Dear ! dear ! it's
very trying being so exalted one day, and ever so
desperate the next—this self-knowledge ! . . ."
" I know what things are good : friendship and
work and conversation. These I shall have. . ."

He tells how the day has brought back to him "that tearing hunger to do and do and do things. I want to walk 1000 miles, and write 1000 plays, and sing 1000 poems, and drink 1000 pots of beer, and kiss 1000 girls, and—oh, a million things! . . . The spring makes me almost ill with excitement. I go round corners on the roads shivering and nearly crying with suspense, as one did as a child, fearing some playmate in waiting to jump out and frighten one. . . ." "Henceforward," writes Mr Marsh in another passage, " the only thing he cared for—or rather he felt he ought to care for—in a man, was the possession of goodness ; its absence the one thing he hated. . . . It was the spirit, the passion that counted with him."

His verse tells the same tale. Life to poetry, poetry to life—that is one of the few virtuous circles. Life and thought to him were an endless adventure. His mind, as he says, was restless as a scrap of paper in the wind. His moods ebbed and flowed, even while his heart, that busy heart, as he called it, was deeply at rest. Wit to such a mind is a kind of safety-valve, or even the little whistle which the small boy pipes up for courage' sake in the dark. Letters and poems flash and tingle with wit—and rare indeed are the poems in our language which, like " Tiare Tahiti," " The Funeral of Youth," and " The Old Vicarage," are witty and lovely at the same time :

> And in that garden, black and white,
> Creep whispers through the grass all night ;
> And spectral dance, before the dawn,
> A hundred Vicars down the lawn ;
> Curates, long dust, will come and go
> On lissom, clerical, printless toe ;
> And oft between the boughs is seen
> The sly shade of a Rural Dean . . .
> Till, at a shiver in the skies,
> Vanishing with Satanic cries,
> The prim ecclesiastic rout
> Leaves but a startled sleeper-out,
> Grey heavens, the first bird's drowsy calls,
> The falling house that never falls . . .

Few poets have mocked and made fun and made beauty like that, all in one breath, and certainly not the childlike visionaries, though one of them knew that even by mere playing the innocent may go to heaven. And beneath Brooke's wit was humour—the humour that is cousin to the imagination, smiling magnanimously at the world it loves and understands.

Byron, too, was witty, mocking, enjoyed turning things inside out and wrong side upwards, picking ideas to pieces, shocking the timid, the transcendental, the spinners of cocoons; but Brooke, unlike Byron, was never sourly sardonic, never morbidly cynical. Simply because he was always testing, analysing, examining, with an intellect bordering as close on his emotions as his emotions bordered on his intellect, he was, again, in Mr Marsh's words, self-conscious, self-examining, self-critical, but never self-absorbed; never an ice-cold egotist, that is, however insistent he may be on his own individuality. More closely than Byron he resembles Mercutio:

> If love be rough with you, be rough with love;
> Prick love for loving, and you beat love down . . .
> If thou art dun, we'll draw thee from the mire
> Of this, sir-reverence love, wherein thou stick'st
> Up to the ears. Come, we burn daylight, ho . . .
> I mean, sir, in delay
> We waste our lights in vain, like lamps by day.
> Take our good meaning, for our judgement sits
> Five times in that ere once in our five wits.

And in his metaphysical turns, his waywardness, his contradictoriness, his quick revulsions of feeling, he reminds us not less—he reminded even himself (in a moment of exultation)—of the younger Donne.

Though "magic" in the accepted sense is all but absent from his verse—the magic that transports the imagination clean into another

reality, that drenches a word, a phrase, with
the light that was never strangely cast even
on the Spice Islands or Cathay, he has that
other poetic magic that can in a line or two
present a portrait, a philosophy, and fill the
instant with a changeless grace and truth.
That magic shines out in such fragments, for
instance, as :

> *Beauty* was there,
> Pale in her black ; dry-eyed ; she stood alone . . .

or

> And turn, and toss your brown delightful head,
> Amusedly, among the ancient Dead ;

or

> And less-than-echoes of remembered tears
> Hush all the loud confusion of the heart :

or

> There are waters blown by changing winds to laughter
> And lit by the rich skies, all day. And after,
>   Frost, with a gesture, stays the waves that dance
> And wandering loveliness. He leaves a white
>   Unbroken glory, a gathered radiance,
> A width, a shining peace, under the night.

What, again, is it but this magic which stills
the heart, gives light to the imagination, in one

of the less well-known, but not the least quiet
and tender of his poems, " Doubts " ?

> When she sleeps, her soul, I know,
> Goes a wanderer on the air,
> Wings where I may never go,
> Leaves her lying, still and fair,
> Waiting, empty, laid aside,
> Like a dress upon a chair . . .
> This I know, and yet I know
> Doubts that will not be denied.
>
> For if the soul be not in place,
> What has laid trouble in her face?
> And, sits there nothing ware and wise
> Behind the curtain of her eyes,
> What is it, in the self's eclipse,
> Shadows, soft and passingly,
> About the corners of her lips,
> The smile that is essential she?
>
> And if the spirit be not there,
> Why is fragrance in the hair?

Above all, Brooke's poems are charged with, and
surrender the magic of what we call personality.
They seem, as we read them, to bring us into a
happy, instant relationship with him, not only
ghostly eye to eye, but mind to mind. They tell
more than even friendship could discover unaided.
They share his secrets with the world—as if a

boy had turned out the contents of his astonishing pockets just before going to bed. They share them, too, in that queer paradoxical fashion which makes a volume of poems a more secure refuge even than one's lawyer, one's doctor, or a priest.

Many of our fellow-creatures—whether we like or dislike them, approve or disapprove—always remain a little mysterious and problematical. Even when they most frankly express themselves, we are conscious that there is still something in them that eludes us, a dream unshared, a reticence unbroken, a fugitive phantom. Have we, indeed, all of us, to the last dim corner and attic, cellar and corridor, explored ourselves? Because of his very candour, because, so to speak, of what he looked like, this was to some extent true of Rupert Brooke. Age, in time, scrawls our very selves upon our faces. Fast-locked the door of our souls may be, but the key hangs in the porch. But youth and delightful manners may be a mask concealing gravity and deep feeling. And what is one's remembrance of that serenely eager, questing face, stilled, as it were, with the phantom of a smile that might have lingered in the countenance of the Sphinx in her younger days, but that of the very embodiment of youth?

We don't often meet people in this world who instantly recall the Golden Age and remind us that the Greek sculptors went to Life for their models. Even Henry James, in his essay on Brooke, not less in its translucency than five fathoms deep, seems to pause Prospero-like before that Ariel whom he had suddenly encountered in the beautiful setting of the Cambridge "backs." With the lingering gusto which an epicure lavishes on a rare old vintage he tastes—tastes again, and all but hesitates for words to express his precise and ultimate reaction; and to suggest that Henry James was ever at a loss for words is to insinuate that the Mississippi might run short of water.

One was just happy in Brooke's company. Guiltily one eyed his gold. Here in laughing, talking actuality was a living witness of what humanity might arrive at when—well, when we tread the streets of Utopia. Happiness is catching. No doubt this admiration sometimes elated him, without his being aware of it. At times, in certain company, it must have been a positive vexation. Admiration is a dense medium though which to press to what treasure may be beyond. Poets, indeed, unlike children, and for their own sake if not for that of others, should be heard and not seen; and it must have been very difficult for this poet to take cover, to lie low. He came; *you* saw; *he* conquered. And after? Like a good child's birthday cake, he was as rich as he looked.

" I never met," wrote to his mother one heaven-sent friend (I mean sent *to* the outskirts of heaven), " I never met so entirely likeable a chap. . . . Your son was not merely a genius; what is perhaps more important, he had a charm that was literally like sunshine." Indeed the good things simply softly shimmered out of him —wit, enthusiasm, ideas, raillery, fun, and that sympathetic imagination concerning everybody and everything that he himself said was the artist's one duty. He had, of course, his own terms—critical, and perhaps at times a little exacting. If he suffered a fool, no more than with the rest of his own generation was it with a guileless gladness. He preferred humanity to be not too stiff, not too stupid, and not too dry. Talk he loved; and when he listened, his mind was in his eyes, " tree whispering to tree without wind, quietly." If he hated, if his sensitiveness wholly recoiled, then that emphatically was the end of the matter.

He confronted his fellow-creatures just like the boy he was, ready to face what and who may come without flinching; smiling lip and steady

eye. One was conscious of occasional shynesses
and silences, even a little awkwardness at times
that was in itself a grace. One was still more
conscious of an insatiable interest and speculation. His quiet gaze took you in; yours couldn't
so easily take him in. These are but my
own remembrances, few, alas, however vivid
and unfading: and even at that they are
merely those of one of the less responsive
sex !

In spite of life's little disillusionments (which,
it is prudent to remember, we may cause as
well as endure); in spite of passing moods of
blackness and revulsion, nothing could be clearer
in his poems, in his letters, and in himself, than
his zest and happiness. Looking back on his
school-life he said that he had been happier than
he could find words to say. What wonder that
at twenty he describes himself as in the depths
of despondency " because of my age " ? And a
little later: " I am just too old for romance."
What does that mean but that he found life so
full and so arresting that he was afraid he might
not be able to keep pace with it ? It was a needless apprehension. The sea was deep beneath
the waves and the foam. If he had lived to
be, let us say, forty, he would have said just
the same thing, though, perhaps, with more

emphasis and more philosophy. He was never to experience that passing misfortune. He flung himself into the world—of men or of books, of thought and affairs—as a wasp pounces into a cakeshop, Hotspur into the fighting. When his soul flourished on Walter Pater and Aubrey Beardsley, he thought it a waste of time to walk and swim. When, together with meat and alcohol, he gave up these rather rarified dainties, and lived, as it is fabulously reported, on milk and honey, it seemed a waste of time to do anything else. He could not be half-hearted. Indeed, in that " tearing hunger to do things "—working, playing, reading, writing, publishing, travelling, talking, socialism, politics—any one thing seemed a waste of time, because meanwhile the rest of life's feast was kept waiting. " What an incredibly lovely, superb world ! " he exclaims. Lovely, superb—what are the precise epithets which we should choose ? Again, " it *is* fun going and making thousands of acquaintances." It must be fun—when you are Rupert Brooke. Frankly, voraciously, that is how he met everything and everybody—from Mrs Grundy to the Statue of Liberty.

The Statue of Liberty reminds me, vividly and happily, of America. Three years ago, the fact that one of the great American Universities had awarded Brooke the first Howland Memorial Prize—" in recognition of an achievement of marked distinction in the field of literature "—passed, comparatively speaking, unnoticed in England. But that award was not merely an academic compliment. The value of a gift is in the spirit of the giver, and this gift of love and admiration was from the heart. The friend—because none worthier to be sent was free—the friend of Brooke's whose privilege it was to go to New Haven formally to receive that prize on Mrs Brooke's behalf, was absolutely unknown there. His name—my name, as a matter of fact—was, alas, no *Sesame*. In New York I went, I remember, to call one day on a very charming friend of Brooke's, to whom he wrote some of his gayest letters. A graceful coloured lift-girl inquired who the caller was. I told her. Whereupon she exclaimed, with a smile all radiant gold and ivory, " Gee whiz! what a name ! " This trifling and immodest digression is only to show just how Mrs Brooke's ambassador stood in the great eye of America. Now, in Brooke's own words, " American hospitality means that with the nice ones you can be at once on happy and intimate terms." I wish I had words to express how true that is—that heedful, self-sacrificing, unbounded kindness. The nice ones indeed were everywhere, for without exception they all knew, or knew of, Brooke. Not that they knew no other contemporary English poet, perhaps even a little better than John Bull does himself—Mr Yeats, Mr Binyon, Mr Masefield, Mr Gibson. But I had but to whisper "R. B."—and the warmest welcome and interest were mine. Now, in nineteen hundred and sixteen that welcome for his sake was not merely of literary significance. The ardour and devotion of those English sonnets of his had gone home, and the home of poetry is world-wide. Never was a true friendship between two countries and nations of such vital importance as that between England and America to-day. Long before the American nation actually " came into " the war, many, many hearts there beat truly with ours. Cousins cannot invariably see eye to eye. But we cannot forget that generous sympathy in the hour when England needed it. Our steady insight and understanding, with as slight an admixture as possible of a peculiar quality of insularity which may be comprehensively described as " God-Almightiness," is the least we can give in return.

I hope it will be no breach of confidence if I quote a few words from a letter I received from a friend in America only the other day, one who knew Brooke's poetry not by hearsay, but by heart. "I dutifully belong," she writes, "to the English-speaking Unions, and am properly interested in various schemes for making the relations between England and America closer. But I may say this to you—I don't want the alliance to result in the least Americanizing of England. I want England to remain 'like her mother who died yesterday';" (she is quoting Edward Thomas, rare poet and rarest friend). "We over here," she continues, "can't have all the simple, lovely and solitary things of which Englishmen write. It helps so much to be able to think of them as they are in England." These are the words of a devotee of England—such devotees as poetry makes and keeps.

But such were the friends that Brooke himself with his poetry, personality and happiness made wherever he went. "Happy," indeed, is the refrain that runs through all his letters. And then, at length, when on his way to the last great adventure of all : ".I have never," he writes, "I have never been so pervasively happy in my life." That is how he opened the door into one's life, and came in. But behind all that we say or do, behind even what we think, is the solitude wherein dwells what we are : and to that solitude he was no stranger, even though it was not what called most frequently for expression. Because each day was so great a tax, however welcome, on mind and body, he sometimes longed for sleep :

> O haven without wave or tide !
> Silence, in which all songs have died !
> Holy book, where hearts are still !
> And home at length under the hill !
> O mother quiet, breasts of peace,
> Where love itself would faint and cease !
> O infinite deep I never knew,
> I would come back, come back to you,
> Find you, as a pool unstirred,
> Kneel down by you, and never a word,
> Lay my head, and nothing said,
> In your hands, ungarlanded ;
> And a long watch you would keep ;
> And I should sleep, and I should sleep !

So, again and again his thoughts in his poetry turn towards death, only in appearance the deepest sleep of all. But then, again, since nothing in life could satisfy such a hunger and aspiration for life, beyond mood and change he longed for a peace " where sense is with knowing one " : and, beyond even this bodiless communion, for the peace that passes understanding :

> Lost into God, as lights in light, we fly,
> Grown one with will.

Simply because things as they are are not as they should be, we take refuge at times from the defeats and despairs of this mortal existence in satire and scepticism, a passing doubt in man, in goodness, in the heavenly power. So, too, did he. He kept piling up the fuel for those " flaming brains " of his ; took life at the flood. When ashes succeeded the blaze and the tide ran low and the mud-flats shimmered in the mocking sunshine ; why, he could at least be frank. Each in turn he accepted life's promises ; when it broke some of them—as it sometimes must in order to keep the others—he closely examined the pieces, whatever the pang. One promise, however, would never have failed him : " There are only three good things in this world : one is to read, one is to write, the other is to live poetry." The last is by far the most difficult, and Mrs Grundy is not un- charmed to discover that not all the poets are masters of the art. But there it is : they are his own deliberate words ; and he meant what he said.

What, if he had lived, he would have *done* in this world is a fascinating but an unanswerable question. This only can be said : that he would have gone on being his wonderful self. Radium is inexhaustible. As we look back across the gulf of these last four years we see him in vividest outline against the gloom. Other poets, beloved of the gods, and not unendeared to humanity, have died young, as did he. Indeed it may be that, however uncompromising the usages of time, every poet, every man in whom burns on a few coals of imagination, " dies young." But no other English poet of his age has given up his life at a moment so signal, so pregnant. This has isolated and set Rupert Brooke apart. No single consciousness can even so much as vaguely realise the sacrifice of mind and hope and aspiration, of life and promise, "lovely and of good report," which this pitiless and abominable war has meant to England and to the world. His sacrifice was representative. The " incantation of his verse " quickened "a new birth," his words were "sparks among mankind."

What place in English literature the caprices of time and taste will at length accord him does not concern us. Let us in our thoughts be as charitable as we can to our posterity, who will have leisure for judgment, and can confer that remembrance which fleeting humanity flatters in the term "immortality."

> I saw him beat the surges under him,
> And ride upon their backs . . .

His bold head
'Bove the contentious waves he kept, and oar'd
Himself with his good arms in lusty stroke
To the shore, that o'er his wave-worn basis bow'd
As stooping to relieve him.   I not doubt
He came alive to land.

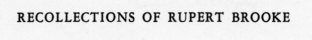

RECOLLECTIONS OF RUPERT BROOKE

RECOLLECTIONS

OF

RUPERT BROOKE

BY

MAURICE BROWNE

Mrs., Mr. and Miss Van Volkenburg have generously put at my disposal for these *Recollections* the Brooke *ana* in their possession; their permission, in particular, to quote freely from the "diary-letters" has been invaluable. The portrait of Rupert Brooke, reproduced as the frontispiece, and the facsimile of his letter appear through the courtesy of Eugene Hutchinson, Chicago.

TO RUPERT BROOKE[1]

I give you glory, for you are dead.
The day lightens above your head;
The night darkens about your feet;
Morning and noon and evening meet
Around and over and under you
In the world you knew, the world you knew.

Lips are kissing and limbs are clinging,
Breast to breast, in a silence singing
Of unforgotten and fadeless things:
Laughter and tears and the beat of wings
Faintly heard in a far-off heaven;
Bird calls bird; the unquiet even
Ineluctable ebb and flow
Flows and ebbs; and all things go
Moving from dream to dream; and deep
Calls deep again in a world of sleep.

There is no glory gone from the air;
Nothing is less. No, as it were
A keener and wilder radiance glows
Along the blood, and a shouting grows
Fiercer and louder, a far-flung roar
Of throats and guns: your island shore
Is swift with smoke and savage with flame;
And a myriad lovers shout your name,
Rupert! Rupert!, across the earth;
And death is dancing, and dancing birth;
And a madness of dancing blood and laughter
Rises and sings, and follows after
All the dancers who danced before,
And dance no more, and dance no more.

You will dance no more; you will love no more;
You are dead and dust on your island shore.
A little dust are the lips where
Laughter and song and kisses were.
And I give you glory, and I am glad
For the life you had and the death you had,
For the heaven you knew and the hell you knew,
And the dust and the dayspring which were you.

1916

When twenty-first-century realists try to disentangle the man from the myth in the "Brooke legend," as it is already called, they will be attempting a difficult task: the man *was* the myth. And the devil of it is that, in this perfectly normal world of war, industrialism, and the daily press, those who subsist by an income cannot believe the truth about Brooke, and those who live by the grace of God cannot tell it. All that we who knew him intimately find to say is that he "was such-and-such a height, had honey-coloured hair, and wrote verses:" if we are wise, we leave it at that and his letters, like Mr. Marsh; else we chatter banally and "in bad taste" about him, like me.

RECOLLECTIONS OF
RUPERT BROOKE

TOGETHER WITH SOME UNPUBLISHED
LETTERS AND VERSES

I

BROOKE and I had been chasing each other for two years across two continents before we finally met. For two previous years, mutual friends had plagued us with mutual tales. In London, in the summer of 1913, I had seen his photograph for the first time: the beauty of the man — I repeat the abysmal mythopoeic phrase: the beauty of the man — astounded me; when I asked who it was, I got heartily damned for my "American" provincialism. At last, early in 1914, coming down to the Chicago Little Theatre one morning, I found a note[2] which he had scribbled there an hour or so before:

DEAR MR. BROWNE,

My friend Harold Monro,—who claims some relationship[3] with you,—and also Eileen Allenby[2] and other people, told me when I passed through Chicago to give you various messages of affection—Are you too busy to receive them? I'm staying at the Auditorium Hotel for a few days—

Yours sincerely
RUPERT BROOKE

Maurice Browne Esq

I telephoned him at once; the Auditorium Hotel is next door to the Fine Arts Building, where the Chicago Little Theatre used to be: and a minute later he was in the theatre.

At the moment of our meeting I happened to be standing on my head[4], no unusual position for a theatre-manager. The humanity of my position — which, in relation to Brooke, has not noticeably changed and is now not likely to — appealed to his sense of fitness in mortal affairs, especially as my mother-in-law, an elderly, white-haired and austere lady, immediately threw her arms round his neck. He promptly kissed my wife, and five minutes later the four of us were marching arm-in-arm down Michigan Avenue to drink beer.

My memory of the next ten days is a riotous blur of all-night talks, club sandwiches, dawns over Lake Michigan, and innumerable "steins." Brooke continued staying at the Auditorium (which he detested), but spent virtually all his time at our theatre—where Mme. Borgny Hammer was then playing *Hedda Gabler* — and at our studio a few blocks south, which overlooked the lake. There he showed us his South Sea treasures and told us of his Gauguin find. I have beside me as I write several chains of tiny South Sea shells, which he gave to Miss Van Volkenburg together with a copy of Belloc's *Four Men*; the latter he knew almost by heart. The three of us would sit up night after night in our studio, talking, singing folk-songs, reading poetry, surging across the tiny room, like happy healthy children. On three successive mornings we saw the sun rise. Miss Van Volkenburg, who is unusually truthful for an actress, assures me that at breakfast, which the three of us ate together every morning about eleven in the Auditorium, he and I were quite adultly cross, ill-mannered and quarrelsome.

One night I remember with peculiar vividness. I had telegraphed Arthur Ficke to tear himself from his desk in Davenport (where he then pretended to practice law), bribing — as is customary — the ascetic attorney with promises of poetry, beer and Brooke. He came, saw and fell. The Johnsonian literary editor of the *Chicago Evening Post*, Llewellyn Jones, that true and disinterested friend of poets, was there with his rectitude, brave platitudes, and sturdy brain; several members of the Chicago Little Theatre Company drifted in after their performance; and, among others who came and went, I remember a woman who was at that time a public librarian in Chicago, one who has given the best years of her life to unobtrusive kindliness and the service of beauty in others, to whom Brooke took an immediate liking: and a lost dog with bad teeth named D——.

D—— had descended on us from the unknown, as, periodically, lost dogs did in those days, from Arizona and

Saskatchewan and the parts about Podunk, for free drinks, a meal or two, and the few dollars they could beg—or occasionally steal—from the theatre's till: one of those lost dogs is in an American prison today — shamefully enough, and the shame is not his — for being an I. W. W.; another, a confessed till-robber, is today a man of affairs on Broadway and operates, with the connivance of the police, a sensationally successful bootlegging-joint in Greenwich Village. Brooke disliked D—— as vigorously, and treated him as kindly, as any of us, but he would not read poetry in his presence. So eventually D—— departed, with others who had come to gape, and the night began. Ficke has celebrated it in his sonnet:

PORTRAIT OF RUPERT BROOKE[5]

One night—the last we were to have of you—
High up above the city's giant roar
We sat around you on the studio floor—
Since chairs were lame or stony or too few—
And as you read, and the low music grew,
In exquisite tendrils twining the heart's core,
All the conjecture we had felt before
Flashed into torch-flame, and at last we knew.

And Maurice, who in silence long has hidden
A voice like yours, became a wreck of joy,
To inarticulate ecstasies beguiled.
And you, as from some secret world now bidden
To make return, stared up, and like a boy
Blushed suddenly, and looked at us, and smiled.

[14]

What the poems were which Brooke read that particular night I have, of course, no recollection (in the course of those ten days we made him read us almost everything he had written,[6] including *Lithuania* and all the South Sea poems, then still in manuscript), but I can vividly see him sitting on the floor — his favourite position — with his knees hunched up, his arms round them, and his back against a wardrobe, blushing — with unfeigned pleasure, not embarrassment — when any of us became peculiarly inarticulate over some special loveliness. Ficke (despite his sonnet: poets are notoriously untruthful) sat in a decrepit rocker, the only chair we boasted, with his long legs infernally in the way, while the rest of us sprawled over the two cots, a table, a packing-case, and what other furniture the room afforded. Brooke read well — much better, of course, than the average professional reader or actor reads poetry — quietly and shyly, with little tone-variation, dwelling slightly on significant vowel-sounds and emphasizing rhyme and rhythm: reading, in fact, as a good lyric poet always reads good lyric poetry, taking care of the sound and letting the sense take care of itself. Occasionally one of us would fall foul of something which another had written—for both Ficke and I read some of our things that night — and the virulence of our mutual criticism made, I learned later, those who were unused to hearing craftsmen discuss each other's work believe that we did not mean what we said.

Brooke had the poet's passion for doing and seeing every-

[15]

thing — he even suffered (not gladly) to be thrown as a lion to the Christians at one of those Sunday afternoon receptions in the Chicago Little Theatre, which delighted our guests so incomprehensibly and so comprehensibly terrified their hosts — and one day, when the strange odour which periodically descends on Chicago from the west was borne in upon him, he snuffed eagerly and departed for the stockyards. We were all hoping that we might arrange to cross the Atlantic together, so Miss Van Volkenburg and I, eager to go east with him from Chicago, dilated on the smells and superlative squalor of Gary. But the rumour of Pittsburgh had reached his ears: even our thrilling account of the infinitely superior monstrosity of middle-western industrial prostitution failed to convince him — he was extraordinarily pig-headed — and, a day or two later, he set his face vitriolically toward Eastern Steel, to study the Feudal System.

As I write, the absurdity of this three-dimensional time-imposture of ours shows all its fantastic stuffiness. Rupert Brooke is walking down Michigan Avenue *now*, his right hand swinging his hat — some broad-brimmed high-crowned ridiculous featherweight, plaited from South Sea straw, of which he was inordinately vain — his long legs striding carelessly and freely, his eyes fixed straight ahead, utterly unconscious of people and things: for he's talking, talking, as only he can talk; were he not talking, not a detail of what was happening about him would be missed. Every woman who passes — and every other man — stops, turns round, to look at that lithe and radiant figure. The wind, the dirty Chicago wind, is blowing Chicago dust and Illinois Central cinders through his hair — longish, wavy, the colour of his skin: a sort of bleached gold, both of them, from the sun of his lagoons, where day after day and month after month he had lived in a loin-cloth, spearing fish, writing poetry, making love. His suit is the colour of his hair. It seems as if the youth of all the world, singing and sun-golden, were, in an unastonished ecstasy and Chicago, tramping the paved side-walks of the City of God.

A few days later he wrote, on New Willard Hotel stationery, from a somewhat different habitation:

> [*Washington, D. C.*]
> Sunday
> May 10 1914

DEAR BROWNE,

I'm leaving this place on Thursday, sooner than I expected, and my ticket seems to compel me to cut out Philadelphia, and other places by the way. So I may be able to get away from these shores sooner than I thought. It would be extraordinarily pleasant for *me,* if I knew there was going to be a couple of people one could exchange ideas with on the boat . . . *Your* view of the situation isn't my affair. But, if you answer, by return, on a card, giving the name and date of sailing of your boat, you'll be running the RISK of me coming on her (especially if she's Atlantic Transport). Don't say you weren't warned.

Isn't it typical of America that the *Auditorium* porter checked all my luggage to Washington, Pennsylvania? Now, if I'd been in England, my luggage wouldn't have gone a thousand miles in the opposite direction. But if it *had,* I should never have seen it again. Whereas, this being America, it has been located and is to arrive here tomorrow. A nation of kindly dreamers.

Urana!
RUPERT BROOKE

I replied from Chicago:

May 13, 1914

DEAR BROOKE,

Deafening cheers and extraordinary hilarity! We sail on the *Philadelphia,* American Line, from New York, on the twenty-ninth. If you don't go with us, now that we have nerved ourselves to the ordeal, we will defame your character—if possible—throughout Europe. I will tell stories in Munich that . . . I think you will come.

Prosit. Auf wiedersehen. Selah.

He answered by return[7]:

New Jersey May 16 [1914]

DEAR BROWNE,

I saw a pamphlet, with illustrations, on the American Line. It seemed clear that most of one's fellow-passengers are of the lowest kind of ruffian. The Atlantic Transport is said by experts to be infinitely preferable. I nearly telegraphed to you that Gilbert Murray was going by the A. T. and wanted us to accompany him. But my public school honesty prevented me. So I took a *suite*[8] on the Philadelphia. If I am unwell all the way, I shall hold you to blame.—

I am becoming infinitely homesick. I have made up

a Litany about all the places I know on the line between Plymouth and London—and they are many. I
shall si[ng] it, rather loudly, all the five hours of that
journey. So perhaps you'd better engage a separate
compartment—What bleedin' fun! We'll pain[t] the
Atlantic red. I suppose you can't bring Raymond
Johnson[9] and Lövborg[10] and the rest along?

I'm *en route* for Bawston. New York about May
22—

c/o Russell Loines
   49 Wall St   herzliche Grüsse
     N. York   R B

The next letter is from New York, from the Hotel
McAlpin:

Monday [*May 25, 1914*]

DEAR BROWNE,

I'll rub along with the gods[11] till Thursday. I'll
meet you then. If I miss you: this is where I am:
God help me. I don't know your taste in hotels.
Mine corresponds with Mr. Arnold Bennett's. But this
is rather cheaper than the Auditorium—

Hutchinson,[12] who has a distressingly modern
mania for photographing the soul instead of the body,
has sent me a lovely reproduction of a beautiful middle aged woman playing a piano, thinking of the
Ewigkeit, in profile, facing the dawn.

"Is *that* the mouth that touched Tahitian lips,
And drained the topless tankards of Berlin?"

No: no! I have not changed so much. I returned
the infamy with a jeer.

One thing, if you have time to think. Do you stock,

[19]

or does Chicago, *Georgian Poetry*?[13] If so, will you buy and bring me two copies. New York has run out of them.

Y . . .

RB

You reach New York on *Thursday*, I'm concluding. *If* its WEDNESDAY, you must wire.

We did reach New York on Thursday; but Brooke had rushed off somewhere for a last American supper, and, as we had an engagement that evening with Mrs. Havelock Ellis, who had been the Little Theatre's guest in Chicago a short time previously, during our production of some of her plays, the three of us did not foregather till the following morning at breakfast. — Two or three weeks later we met Mr. Ellis in London, with the message from his wife that American newspapers, which she, in common with Brooke and ourselves, had had to endure, were seldom bothered by a little thing like the truth. Mr. Ellis will, I hope, forgive me for betraying the reason he has never visited America: he cannot face the American press. Strange as American journalists think it, sensitive people shrink from their caresses.

At breakfast Miss Van Volkenburg, Brooke and I were busy comparing notes on American hotels; he and I found ourselves in substantial agreement, although, incomprehensibly, Miss Van Volkenburg expressed herself as unwilling to exchange permanently the private baths, bright rooms, and telephone service of the American hotel, for the red plush curtains, seductive bellropes, and richly varied roast mutton, which have made English hostelries famous.

Just before the *Philadelphia* sailed, Miss Van Volkenburg wrote in her diary-letter home: "Rupert Brooke is looking very fit and Rupertish, and is carrying a straw hat, an overcoat, Hutchinson's photographs, some magazines, books and a writing-case! His arrival on board created a *succès de scandale*. Thus are we English[14] made!"

Across the top of this letter he has scrawled:

ave atque vale!

RUPERT BROOKE

II

Miss Van Volkenburg's diary-letters home tell the story of the voyage.

"May 30 [1914]

". . . The day has been quite wonderful — cold with a stiff breeze but beautifully clear and oh! so fresh; I feel as if I had never really breathed air before.

"We have a nice place for our three chairs, beside the railing that used to divide the first from the second class;[15] Mr. Brooke and I slept in them most of the afternoon — and our faces are now as red as the curtains in the state-rooms. After dinner we played three-handed bridge with Mr. Brooke and then walked round the deck . . . There are more nationalities on board than I've ever encountered simultaneously before: French, heaps of them; some German; English; and an Indian chief who wears a bead band round his head with a feather stuck in it — a lovely person . . .

"*May 31*

". . . There are millions of people on board (among them 30 members of the University of California Glee Club) dressed in all sorts and conditions of clothes, and they walk round and round the deck until one grows dizzy watching them. Their watchword is, 'This is my *seventh — tenth — fourteenth* lap!' said in a *very* shrill voice. Then the Glee Club Boys burst into song, 'You are my sun, won't you adore me?' and stop short in the middle of a verse to argue or suggest a drink, so that one never discovers whether the love is finally requited. — There is a small fat girl whom Mr. Brooke calls 'the pig-child', and I silently shudder, wondering what he would have called me in the old days . . .

"*June 1*

". . . It is raining — little drizzly raindrops, as if they didn't care much about coming; I don't either, for they've driven us away from our precious railing on deck near the Marconi house where the machine is spitting forth messages like millions of angry bees. The poor little pig-child is sitting on her father's lap looking most disconsolate, and every one else has departed . . . We haven't talked with anyone at our table except our own four[16] selves, but next Mr. Hargreave sits a tiny, tiny old maid who looks like an unfeathered sparrow just accidentally fallen from her nest; next her is an ugly man with a squint and a lame leg, who must be interesting;[17] next him is a Roman Catholic priest who looks nice and holy; across from him is another Roman Catholic priest who looks nice and jolly — somewhat on the order of the pig-child; next him is a small thin man who passes the butter and bread and things: when the steward asked him to change his seat and move next Don,[18] saying 'You're not particular, are you?' he answered hastily, 'Not at all'. The steward is delightful — as they always are — and tells us that lor luv us eel do evrythink e ken feh rus buh they *har* seh slow ih the kitching—naw like is lawst boat, the Herlympic, were evrythink wuz wytin ready feh yeh. He never remembers exactly what people order and always brings an extra ice-cream, which Mr. Brooke, with the air of a martyr and the look of a wicked baby, eats with equal layers of rhubarb and sugar. The English sense of the fitness of food is amazing . . .

"*June 2*

"It has been a *wonderful* day, a Mediterranean day: the water deep blue with a carpet of silver gauze and the sky like Dorothy Fuller's[19] eyes — clearly enigmatical . . . The sun has sunk in an absolutely cloudless sky: a steamer has passed on the horizon: we have seen some more porpoises: and, there being nothing else to see, we have come in for our regular evening occupation [*three-handed bridge*]. Last evening there was a dance, but, needless to say, we didn't participate. There are two young sisters on board, whom Mr. Brooke has named Mimi and Fifi; they are probably about twenty and twenty-two, but they wear their hair in loose curls down their backs, have their skirts to their shoe tops and their eyes on every man in sight — several hundreds. The younger — Mimi — is quite the most luscious little sweetmeat I've yet seen; last evening, as Don and I were sitting demurely on a bench looking at the moon, I heard her tones raised in a weakly protesting 'Oh George!' We turned and saw George silhouetted against that decent self-respecting moonlight in a torrid embrace which lasted until Don and I got bored and went to bed. — Mr. Brooke is having sighs and eyes cast at him; even a married woman took a snapshot of him today, because he has 'such a noble head.' A young girl two tables down from us gazes at him, awestruck and beautifully melancholy. When I told him of her adoration, he remarked 'How dull.' How we women suffer!

"*June 3*

"A nasty, ducky, day — cold, drizzly, and very windy . . . We have been gazing on maps of London, and I find them more bewildering than ever . . .

"Mr. Brooke told me a conversation that he had overheard in the library today; at least he vowed he had and pointed out the alleged conversationalists. A sad-looking English officer was sitting at a table sorting papers, when he was joined by a loquacious lady who asked him where he was going and why; importuned sufficiently, he told her that he was going home to England on account of the death of his little son, who had run through a French window and cut his throat so severely that he had bled to death; instantly and sympathetically the lady responded: 'I know *just* how you feel, because I lost a large diamond ring two weeks ago.' — I'm scribbling hurriedly, for in a moment I am going to hear three immortal sonnets written respectively by Maurice Browne, Rupert Brooke and Ronald Hargreave, to *bouts rimés*; they were composed between the hours of five and six fifteen, and, every time I approached the trio, someone would look up and say 'sssh!' solemnly, so now I await the result . . .

"Tell Raymond [*Jonson*] that Mr. Hargreave has been experimenting — some of it here on shipboard for our benefit — in *projecting* scenery, by painting a landscape on glass, putting it in a kodak in place of the film, then setting an electric bulb back of it and throwing the reflection on a big piece of paper some distance ahead — very much after Don's theory. Don, Mr. Brooke and I have been in his (Mr. Hargreave's) cabin most of the day, working on it, and we're all very pleased and excited . . .

"They haven't read the sonnets: I think they're afraid!
"*June 4*
"This has been another grey and rather windy day; stormy and a bit misty — not enough for the fog-horn, thank goodness, and not too cold to sit on deck. We —

Mr. Brooke and I — installed ourselves in our corner, while Don went off to his writing. We sit facing the stern with our backs haughtily turned to the rest of our fellow-passengers, who wander past and eye Mr. Brooke with elaborate carelessness. He was in fine form, telling stories of the great and near-great for about three hours, with just the slightest touch of frosty snobbishness. I grew so interested in watching him that at times I forgot to listen. When he finished a story, he would set his eyes ahead until the queer little cast came in one of them, run his fingers through his hair with ferocious energy, pause, grasp his nose between his thumb and fore-finger, tweak it gently two or three times (you know that 'quirky' way of his), stop, pull his Jaeger blanket high around his head (leaving none of it to protect his legs), and start on some fresh recollection. He told me a delightful story about Henry James, which ran something like this: Mr. James, coming out of a Bond Street bookshop in an abstracted mood, ran into a most aristocratic lady about to enter her victoria; shocked at his awkwardness, he began an apology, but, as a simple 'I beg your pardon' failed to express his exact shade of feeling, he leapt on the step of the carriage as it moved off and began again; his second attempt proving no better than his first, he clung to the step and tried once more; his third attempt was no more fruitful; so he rode on, clinging to the carriage-door with one hand, holding his hat in the other, with his coat-tails streaming in the breeze. As they reached the Marble

Arch, he formed a perfect sentence of nine lines, asked permission to descend, and departed . . .

"We have relaxed our frigid exclusiveness in favour of two charming young girls from New York, Ethel and Frances P——; even Don likes them, and I caught a sudden glimmer in both his and Mr. Brooke's eyes, when Ethel quoted *The Crock of Gold* . . . As we began our evening ritual tonight, I looked up, saw three girls' faces at the library port-hole, and heard one of them say wistfully, as she gazed at Mr. B., 'Do they always play three-handed?'

"Here are two of the immortal sonnets: Mr. Hargreave threw his overboard, and I had to grab Don and Mr. Brooke to prevent their jumping after it.

THE TRUE BEATITUDE[20]

They say, when the Great Prompter's hand shall ring
    Down the Last Curtain upon earth and sea,
    All the Good Puppets have Eternity
To praise their God, worship and love and sing,
Or, to the walls of Heaven wandering,
    Look down on those damned for some fretful d——,
    Mock them (all theologians agree
On this reward for virtue), laugh, and fling

New sulphur on the sin-incarnadined . . .
    —Ah, Love! still temporal, and still atmospheric,
    Teleologically unperturbed,
We share a peace by no divines divined,
An earthly garden hidden from any cleric,
    Untrodden of God, by no Eternal curbed.

PLATO WAS RIGHT

When Wagner, drunk with music, belched the *Ring,*
    He had not for excuse the emetic sea;
    Time did not lengthen to eternity,
Nor drive him, like us wretched men, to sing
Endless rhymed-endings. (Rupert, wandering,
    Stares seaward; Ronald growls an angry d——;
    Both scratch their heads, and hiccough; and I agree:
Villainous verse, and wine, not fit to fling
Even to the fishes). He wasn't incarnadined
    With shipboard claret; he sat by atmospheric
    And philadelphic victuals unperturbed;
He could walk dry land, and chuckle; he wasn't divined
    By a fat divine, nor scowled on by a thin cleric . . .
    And yet he sang. Pegasus should be curbed.

"There is a concert in progress in the dining-saloon, where the thirty Glee Club Boys from California are singing to all the multitude except Rupert Brooke, Don and myself. *We* are sitting in magnificent and lonely state in the library, writing such exquisite ballads as this,[21] and drinking beer and lemonade.

    Sing not of California, no!
    Nor of nothin' else, O woe!
    Damn you, be dumb.
    For some, God wot, have voices rare: but some
    Know not when golden silence should
    Sink like a drowsy bird within the wood,
    That twitters once, before the night, and then,
    Head under wing, leans up against his hen
    And shoves her off the branch. They hush their
        laughter . . .

> So silence follows song, and sleep comes after—
> Sleep of the evening: would that it came faster!
> (Again she sings: God blast her).

"Isn't it *beautiful*? You can see clearly that the two men didn't appreciate my levity[22] . . . We have finished our evening bridge and will soon take our turn around the deck and then go to bed. The Olympic passed us in all her glory this morning about eight; she would be sharply defined for a moment, then the mist would slowly drop over her and leave only a dim mass against the sky . . .

"We expect to reach Plymouth about 6:30 tomorrow evening . . . 'Eddie' Marsh, a friend of Mr. Brooke's and Eileen Allenby's, has just sent Mr. Brooke a marconigram (!) asking the three of us to dine with him and Eileen at his flat tomorrow night, but we, of course, wouldn't get there in any case, and poor Mr. Brooke can't: he is *rather* distressed!

"*June 5*

"It is about 10:45 of our last morning on board: always a sad day when it's been a good voyage; this has—except for my back,[23] which at least has made me picturesque, for I have always had my pillow put on my chair first, and then Don has cautiously lowered me into it, while Mr. Brooke has watched with immense indifference, and everyone has looked and whispered, 'Aren't they nice?' 'What's the matter with her?' And I've had a smypathetic stewardess to bring me my breakfast of orange, pulled bread and coffee, and talk to me in low, soothing, English tones, and altogether I've felt like some wounded Queen! — I'm sitting on the deck with Mr. Brooke near the prow, with Don's fur rug and my pillow under me, and another blessed rug over me; our chairs seem to have dropped overboard, and trunks — heaps of them — have taken their places. By the way, the mattresses in our berths, which I thought were feather, are air: we were in our cabin with Mr. Brooke, and the steward, who was fixing it, suddenly turned to him and said: 'These ere mattresses! Yeh cawnt get henny hair hintoo em. Hi doan mean the air uv yer ead, Hi mean the hair uv the hatmosphere.' Mr. Brooke behaved nobly, but Don precipitately vanished.

"Our table steward has nearly sent the three of us into hysterics—he's tall and square, his hair is black and square, so are his eyes, and he smiles bewilderedly when we go off into meaningless paroxysms of laughter. The other day Don said, 'I'll have pineapple fritters and queen's cake, please.' The steward paused, opened his mouth, closed it, and then gasped horrifiedly, 'One's cold—an' the other's 'ot, sir!' Whereat Don and Mr. Brooke exploded, and the steward departed in wounded dignity to bring the queen's cake and the pineapple fritters . . .

"We're almost in. Land was sighted a long time ago, and we can smell new-mown hay! Mr. Brooke is leaning over the taffrail, sniffing ecstatically. A few moments ago, as I was standing there beside him, suddenly we heard an awful

se behind us; our heads turned sharply — and *click* went
odak, amid laughter and apologetic smiles. A little later
voman came up to the three of us, and rather embar-
sedly asked who we were; we rather embarrassedly
lied, 'Bro ok e'; whereupon she said that she was asking
 a friend of hers, 'who simply *had* to know, for we
ked *quite* the most interesting people on board, and
ply *wouldn't* talk to anyone else, and seemed to have
h a good time.' We assured her that we did — and were!
The sea-gulls are flying around and around the boat;
 smell of the land is glorious; and everything is hurry —
ry — hustle — bustle. Mr. Brooke has found out that
 [*Russian*] Ballet is in London, so we may not go to
is.

'Here's a 'threnody'[24] for Mr. Hargreave that Mr. Brooke
 just written; the steward came up and solemnly gave
 B. a note from Mr. H., in which he (Mr. H.) said that
was so ashamed of his sonnet that he had jumped over-
rd.

    I. M.   R. H.   June 5 — 1914
  The world's great painter-soul, whom we deplore,
  Loved California much, but music more.
  His verse—but hush! the poor man's dead and gone.
  What Fifi lost the mermaidens have won.

une 6, dawn

We're on land—blessed blessed land. We saw Mr.
ke off about midnight — in wild spirits; we're to meet

him in town next week. Marsie (Don's mother) arrived about 4 this morning, and of course we sat up for her, so — once again — we've not been to bed all night. We didn't get in until after nine last evening, but the sun was setting and the approach to Plymouth as we came into the harbor was amazingly beautiful; that harbor is *the* most lovely thing I have ever seen. The smell of the new-mown hay came in great waves to us, the whole evening was full of that English radiance, my two menfolk were dancing and shouting like schoolboys — and oh! when we stepped on land, I realized for the first time how unconsciously one dreads the sea: we had heard rumors of the fate of the *Empress of Ireland* just before we sailed, but nothing definite was given us on shipboard; it was only as we landed that we actually knew the facts: *horrible,* isn't it?—As I write this, I can turn my head and look over the water; the sun is rising, the sea is a mass of white and blue and purple and green; all around me the birds are singing, and the whole world seems so sweet and kind and harmless. How radiant it all is!"

III

FOR two or three days after landing, the mere fact of being home, in England, breathing deep breaths of English air, was an ecstasy obliterating thought. Brooke rushed up to London and on to his mother's house at Rugby; my mother

drove Miss Van Volkenburg and myself to Dartmoor to
eat Devonshire cream; thence to Exeter and Salisbury, where
we listened to many-century-old antiphonies and trod many-
century-old lawns: and on to Stonehenge, where at nightfall
among the haunted pillars we watched for the tragic shape
of Tess. We reached London early the following week, to
find a letter from Brooke waiting for us:

<blockquote>

24 Bilton Road   Sunday [*June 7, 1914*]
Rugby

DEAR BROWNE,

Marsh had already got tickets for me and him for
the Ballet on *Thursday*. So I am coming up to Town
on Wednesday or Thursday. I suppose you'll very
likely be going to the Ballet that night. But wherever
you are, you'll be free at 11:15 p. m. For that's when
our supper party at Marsh's begins. Eileen's coming—
who else, I don't yet know. Millions of lovely people.
For further particulars, I refer you to Eileen, (who is
nice, though old and ugly.[25]) Leave news of your
whereabouts with her or the Poetry Bookshop, if you
haven't time to write.

(By the way, any letters from Germany, about the
German theatrical things, astonishingly waiting for
you at the P. B. will be by my command. But there'll
likely be none.)

Go to Boris Godunov
Go to Whitechapel
Go to Prinz Igor
Go to Hell

Britanically

R B

</blockquote>

At the bottom of this letter is a pen and ink drawing, rather in the style of Mr. Wells' illustrations to his own novels, of a Union Jack *rampant*.

We followed all these injunctions except the last, substituting, unwisely, for the place recommended, a famous hostelry in Oxford Street: Eileen Allenby, the Ballet, and London after two years saved us from it, however, for eighteen hours out of the twenty-four. Meanwhile Brooke's mind was busy with the party:

24 Bilton Road   Tuesday
Rugby   June 9 [*1914*]

DEAR BROWNE,

I hope Thursday night's all right: Marsh has asked Norman Wilkinson, and Rothenstein, and Eileen, and I believe Henry Ainley and a lot of mimes—It should be great fun. He seemed to think Abercrombie couldn't come up that night. (Abercrombie's in Surrey) But he'll get him for lunch next day, *Friday* if you two are free to lunch with him and me, at 1:45. If you *are,* will you post the enclosed letter [*to Abercrombie*]?

When are you in Birmingham?

I come to London Thursday morning to Saturday. Salve!

ever—

R B

I thought of going to Prince[26] Igor on Friday. Did you?

We did. With London and all our friends calling, Miss Van Volkenburg and I decided to postpone our journey

[34]

to the Continent for ten days. Mrs. Brooke invited us to Rugby, but we couldn't tear ourselves from town, and, on Thursday afternoon, Brooke met us there; we had dinner with him and Marsh, and went with Brooke and Miss Allenby to the Ballet (*Les Papillons* and *Petrushka*), where we gazed with wide and disappointed eyes on George Moore, Queen Alexandra, Arnold Bennett, and Mr. & Mrs. Bernard Shaw ("What a disillusion", Miss Van Volkenburg's diary-letter exclaims; "he looked like a very solemn English clergyman, she round and small and motherly. And I thought Shaw must be romantically unhappy!"). Afterwards the four of us went to Marsh's rooms in Gray's Inn, where "millions of lovely people" were gathered — Norman Wilkinson and Alfred Rothenstein and "a lot of mimes": Granville Barker and Lillah McCarthy and Henry Ainley and Basil Dean; and — I think — Harold Monro and Wilfrid Gibson; in fact all the loveliest people in London: that is to say in the world before the war. But Marsh's cook, whom he stole, like Prometheus, from the ambrosial kitchens of heaven, so bewitched my senses with frozen nectar — called, for some inscrutable reason, iced coffee — that my only memories of that historic night are Brooke solemnly dancing a South Sea Island dance with Jane (I remember nothing of her except her name, her red hair and mouth, and her white enamelled face) over the nibbled (or mown) grass of Gray's Inn, while dawn broke among the sooty trees . . . and a taxi in the early, early morning,

[35]

filled with the loveliest dozen of all those millions, all unaccountably eager to take the others home first, and all "drunk, but not with wine".

The London of the Russian Ballet and the years immediately preceding the war had a peculiar fascination: I remember — although the memory has no special right of entry here, except as giving a picture of that outer world in which Brooke lived and moved — a night at and after the Ballet in the summer of 1913. It was the first performance in London of *Le Sacré du Printemps,* and Karsavina had been her greatest, than which, in female dancing, there is no greater; the stalls were indifferent or hostile, but we in the gallery went mad: we stood on our seats, and waved our hats, and shouted, and the stalls looked up at us with contempt. It was the kind of scene one reads of but seldom sees in the theatre; I have seen it only three other times perhaps: when Duse first played *Francesca da Rimini* in Milan (or it may have been Turin) in the winter of 1900-1901; when Bolm and Carpenter and Robert Edmond Jones achieved their triumph of collective creation with *The Birthday of the Infanta* at the Lexington Theatre in New York some nineteen winters later; and again in New York, some two years after that, when Margaret Anglin at the Manhattan Opera House played the *Iphigenia in Aulis,* a production in which I had the honour and good fortune to have a hand. — After we had, at last, allowed the tired dancers to bow their last farewell, we adjourned — "we", if I remember aright, being Miss Van Volkenburg, my sister, Monro, Gibson, and myself — to the Poetry Bookshop, where in the old Georgian house in the murderous slum, during the next hour, intellectual and near-intellectual London gathered, mostly from the Ballet. That summer Miss Van Volkenburg, Gibson and I were living under the eaves of the Bookshop, and almost nightly a controversy raged between our visitors and us over Eppstein's *Christ*, of which there was a copy in Monro's living-room downstairs. This night, to Eppstein's new vision had been added Stravinsky's, and their combined onslaught on Philistia pounded to fury those who were set in their artistic ways — of whom there has never been a scarcity, whether in London in 1913, or in New York in 1927. The stalls and the gallery surged with bitter words up and down the narrow stairs, *Christ* had to be rescued hastily and indiscriminately from his opponents and exponents alike, and I from the sister of an eminent British novelist, lately deceased, who was threatening Stravinsky in my unworthy person with her umbrella.

But to come back to Brooke and the following summer. The Granville Barkers asked the three of us to tea the next day [June 12]; but Miss Van Volkenburg and I had promised to spend the afternoon with Havelock Ellis. Shy with a shyness more intense even than our own, he took us to a vast eating-house near Piccadilly Circus, where the roar of a band, dishes, and many masticating, saved us from the folly of words, until the fact that we were — actually

—guests of so wise and great a man had grown almost credible. Afterwards, drinking tea, when the band and the feeders had departed, we spoke of America and Mrs. Ellis, and watched his stooped scholarly figure moving noiselessly to fill our wants; it seemed not merely fitting, but inevitable, that the books of so gentle and lovely a human being should once have been burned by the common hangman.

The following afternoon Miss Van Volkenburg, Brooke and I had lunch with the Barkers in a restaurant near the Kingsway Theatre, which Barker was then directing. My recollections of that luncheon are again irrelevant and happy things: Barker's mother, who was his guest of honour, beaming with pride in her son; the head waiter's reverence; Miss McCarthy insisting on a peacock to walk behind her in their next production, because its tail would be so effective; the turned heads of diners at adjacent tables; Miss Van Volkenburg's wide soft brown eyes; and Brooke, for once outshone, crumbling his bread in a slightly jealous silence. (My memory, I daresay, does him wrong; I hope not: the memory is a fascinating and boyish one). For myself, then as now, men and women who had done fine things were my heroes: my love of Brooke would have been a lesser thing, had my admiration for Barker been less; and I am glad of that hero-worship of my early thirties for the man who has since written *The Secret Life* and the man who had already written *Retrospect*.

Brooke, Marsh and Lascelles Abercrombie met Miss Van

Volkenburg and myself for dinner on Friday evening at Simpson's. Abercrombie — a small, dark, shy man, with spectacles and straight, slightly greasy-looking hair — wore, I remember, a queer little green hat which tipped up preposterously in front: his intellectual power, the power of one of the best brains in England, lying unobviously, under it, like Bolshevism under Bond Street in 1914. He and I knew each other rather well "by proxy and correspondence", but had not met personally before; nor, I learn from the *Memoir* (page 145), had Abercrombie and Brooke: they saw each other that day for the first time; yet, although Brooke and I had spoken of Abercrombie and his work many times, it never occurred to me, until the *Memoir* was in my hands, that they were not old friends: Brooke's genius for friendship had nothing in common with the hypotheses of time and place.

After dinner Marsh left us, and, picking up Gibson (and, I think, Monro) on our way, we went again to the Ballet, where we sat (in the gallery, of course) directly behind Lennox Robinson, for the second night that week finding ourselves, by the grace of Celtic or Slavonic gods, next to this gentle maker of plays. The magic of the Russians left us all too thrilled and happy for bed, and once more we adjourned to Marsh's till dawn.

It may have been that night, it may have been another— my memory of those days in London in that summer of 1914 is a phantasmagoria of music and talk and colour and dance and "lovely people", and, though Miss Van Volkenburg's diary-letters are dithyrambic, they do not always give details of dates; if Brooke went back to Rugby next day, as I think he did, it must have been on that night—that he and Abercrombie and Monro and Gibson talked metaphysics at each other and me in Marsh's rooms the night through: Marsh, discreetly, had gone to bed when we came in. Brooke's grasp and handling of intellectual abstractions was much more than unusual, but he was a child in the philosophical hands of Abercrombie, perhaps the most compelling, conversationally, of contemporary British metaphysicians: Brooke did not nibble at the edges of life, but Abercrombie bit clean and straight at the core. I suppose there was no happier group of men in London that night, none with greater capacity for happiness or exercising it more keenly, and, at the same time, no group more aware of the tragic foundations of happiness. While we were young men (our average age could hardly have exceeded 32), none of us — and certainly not Brooke, though he was the youngest — took any of the young man's romantic pleasure in the contemplation of human misery: actuality was actual to us all. It is true that later, as will be told in its time, the great and all-too-actual tidal-wave of human misery swept Brooke and myself apart; but most would say that it was I whom that wave wrecked: nor would I care to contradict them; nor do I think that, even then, his romanticism—as some have called it—was other than youth hurt past bearing by a cataclysm past understanding. The sane and fundamental strength of character in him, his tragic grasp of life, discount, in my judgment, the opinion of those who hold that his best work had been done.

Two days later (on Monday morning, June 15) Miss Van Volkenburg and I went from Eastbourne, where we had spent the week-end with my mother, to Birmingham, to visit its Repertory Theatre, then—and, for all I know, now—the best-equipped theatre of its size, perhaps of any size, in England. John Drinkwater, the remaining co-author of *New Numbers* (as he was then known) — a tall-seeming, dark, handsome man, with a detached and half-humourous manner more American than English — greeted us at the train; he and I again had known each other "by proxy and correspondence" for a number of years, but again had not met personally. We went directly to the theatre, of which Barry Jackson showed us every corner with concealed and proper pride, and thence to the Midland Hotel; there we were joined by Brooke, who had come from Rugby to see us, and by the first Mrs. Drinkwater, a refreshing hoyden (I trust she will take my description as the compliment intended), who sparred with Brooke unmercifully. We had lunch at the hotel as Brooke's guests and afterwards sat in the lounge, drinking what passes in England for coffee and talking, talking, of all the "wonderful and exciting" events which had happened during the preceding forty-eight hours. Miss Van Volkenburg, Brooke and Drinkwater fell finally into a violent argument on "projected" scenery, with which the Birmingham people were also experimenting, and we returned to the theatre, Miss Van Volkenburg and I rather yellow and green at its glories but determinedly encouraged by Brooke with repeated assurances: "Oh — well — pooh! *Some* day — maybe — even in America . . ."

Early in the morning Miss Van Volkenburg and I caught a train for Oxford, to visit the Gilbert Murrays. Much of their talk was of Brooke, as it had been when we visited them in Cromer the previous year; their hopes for him were great.

My casual and irreverent habit of portraiture, unfitted for a Havelock Ellis, would also be unfitted for the Murrays; but they will both, I know, chuckle with me at my memory of two moments. In Cromer Mr. Murray and I had gone for a walk: it rained; on our return Lady Mary reproached God and me with delicacy but infinite concern: I had "let Gilbert get his feet wet". At lunch in Oxford Miss Van Volkenburg and Mr. Murray forgot deliciously cooked chicken for the *Medea*; finally Lady Mary was moved to remonstrance: "Even if she *was* virtuous, she has been dead a long time; this fowl may have had no morals, but it *is* fresh."

A few hours after our return, a day or two later, to my mother's house at Eastbourne, there was a letter, full of European plans for us, from Brooke:

[42]

24 Bilton Road   Tuesday evening
    Rugby   [*June 16, 1914*]

DEAR BROWNE,

Here's the letter to Clotilde von Derp, whose
private name is Clotilde von der Planitz. She speaks
a little English: her mother speaks it well.

In Berlin, if you want any information of *any* kind,
ring up—or get the hotel to ring up,—
                Dudley Ward
                Berlinerstrasse 100
                Charlottenburg—
He'll love to hear from you; say I told you to ring
him up. He'll know all about the theatres, without
holding a brief for any particular gang. See him
if you *want* to, of course: he and his wife are charming: and Clothilde[26] *may* be with them. But you said
you had a lot of people to see.

When you reach Munich send a card to
                Frau Dr. Ewald
                Holzhausen
                Ammersee
                Bayern—
saying I told you to see if she was going to be in
Munich, while you're there. (Holzhausen is 40 miles
away.) She's often in. She is 45, a paintress, very
kindly, speaks perfect English, and has a passion for
Cambridge people. She knows all the *Simplicissimus*
people, so she could show you a jolly side of Munich.

Give any of all these people my love.

There is said to be an exhibition of theatrical design
at Cologne (or Düsseldorf). If there *is,* it will be
very good, and worth taking in [*it was*]. Find out

from Ward in Berlin. (Perhaps Barker knows about it.)

You may infer from all this, that I'm not going to be in London by Thursday morning.[27] You are strangely, terribly, right. My dentist's claims are supreme. I *shall* be in town by Thursday afternoon; so if you're fortunately deferring departure till Friday, I'll yet be at the train with roses and tears. If you *are* staying till then, send a card to me at Marsh's—

If not—we shall meet again: either in this world, or in the next world, or in America. If in this world, we will drink and argue, and your wife shall write us some of her delightful *bout-rimé* sonnets. If in the next world—why, I've little hope of drink, but there'll surely be argument; and whether there are *bouts-rimés* or not—the wise disagree. But we can plan superb light effects with a Fortuny apparatus in the Empyrean, and God himself will work innumerable dimmers for us, and never a hitch.

I had fun in Chicago, on the Atlantic, and in London. I hope you did. When you're safe in Italy, and at peace, send me a card saying what good things Europe showed you. Love to you both— Farewell, lebwohl, talefa, χαίρετε, valete—

RUPERT

We postponed our departure from England for another twenty-four hours. Brooke rejoined us in London on Thursday afternoon; the three of us and Miss Allenby had dinner together that evening and talked far into the night. By the time we were "safe in Italy", peace had left the world.

IV

A WEEK or two later we reached Berlin at eight one morning; it was our first visit there, and we had intended to stay a fortnight. Brooke warned us of what the city was, but our anticipation had not conceived the reality, and, failing to reach Dudley Ward and Clotilde von Derp, we fled from Imperial Prussianism at five the same day. In Munich we got in touch with Frau Dr. Ewald, who invited us to stay with her at Holzhausen, but our theatrical duties compelled us to leave Bavaria before we could accept the invitation. We were in Venice when the storm broke and reached America some two months later. A few weeks afterwards two letters from Brooke arrived almost simultaneously:

Anson Battalion
Second Naval Brigade
Oct. 22 [*1914*]   Betterhanger Camp
Eastry
Kent

MY DEARS,

The world's changed a bit since we were together, hasn't it?

I'm a naval sublieutenant (for service on land). We went to Antwerp, just too late. I saw a city bombarded, and a hundred thousand refugees, and sat in the trenches, and marched all night and did other topical and interesting things. Now we're back for more training. I'll probably get out again by Christmas, and then stay till peace or a kindly shell releases me. I think we're in for another two years.

[45]

The Muses—they're fled. Interned in America and other neutral countries, I hear.

There's nothing to say, except that the tragedy of Belgium is the greatest and worst of any country for centuries. It's ghastly for anyone who liked Germany as well as I did. Their guilt can never be washed out. I'm afraid fifty years won't give them the continunity and loveliness of life back again. I hadn't thought such a thing possible—for a neutral nation. I mean, France, we, Germany, or Russia, are great, and have to expect the consequences of it. But Belgium! . . .

Most people are enlisting. Tom and the other Nesbitt have gone into Cavalry and Artillery. I'm here: among my fellow officers being Denis Browne one of the best young musicians in England; Kelly, the pianist who won the Diamond Sculls; one of the Asquiths; Cherry, who has been secretary to the Berensons in Florence, a man who has been mining in the Soudan; a New Zealander—an Olympic swimmer—; an infinitely pleasant American youth called Dodge, who was hurriedly naturalized "to fight for Justice"— . . . and a thousand more oddities.

In the end, those of us who come back will start writing great new plays. Meanwhile, there's this. Won't Maurice join us?

I'm instituting enquiries about my play.[28] If I can find a copy, I'll send it you out.

I hope you enjoyed your tour in our peaceful Europe.

God be with you both
RUPERT

The second letter was on Royal Naval Barracks, Chatham, stationery:

Anson Battalion
2nd Naval Brigade

October 27 1914

DEAR MAURICE,

I forgot one thing in my letter of four days since. If you meet anyone very keen on the English cause, who owns a very good pair of field-glasses,† give him my name and address as a good and dashing young officer to lend them to, for the war. I lost mine—with the rest of my belongings—in Antwerp: and there are no more *Zeiss* left in England. If you're near a good shop, too, you might enquire if they've got any left in the U. S.

It might prove worth while to send over for a lot of them.

Barracks! What extraordinary new experiences the world holds, even for anyone so elderly as

Yours—ὑμέτερος

Gaily
RUPERT

†Zeiss for preference

I had not money enough to buy a lens, let alone a pair of *Zeiss,* and I could not beg any until December 3, when I was able to write to Brooke that a friend of his, the Countess Capponi, had turned up at the theatre and was forwarding him the *Zeiss,* "of which she happened to have a pair: she seemed sent directly by providence as a source of supply!" In the same letter, urging him to take what care he could of himself, I told him also that I was not going to enlist:

"My place, so far as I can judge, is here, and my job, again so far as I can judge, is to keep the eyes of the people about me on the things which will matter after the war and on the eventual reconstruction."

Soon afterwards, a reply came, written on the Hood Battalion, Royal Naval Division, stationery:

January 26 1915   Blandford
                                   Dorset.

My Dear Maurice,

I liked hearing from you. This is but a line: to ask you to address this to the divine and aureate Harriet.[29] I forget her address. And she is not in the Navy List.

I wrote, under pressure of military labours, some honest but too crude stuff[30] for N. N.[31] and I want to get gold for it from the Yanks, too.

Come over and fight when you get bored with the theatre. England's slowly waking, and purging herself of evil things. It's rather a wonderful sight.

I've to stay here training another two months or three: longer than I expected: because, although *we're* ready for Active Service, the rest of the Division isn't, and we must wait for it. The Camp lies between Eastbury House, where George Bubb Doddington lived, and Badbury Rings, where Arthur defeated the Saxons. And on the chalk down where our huts are, was a Roman Camp once, and a Celtic, before that, and before *that,* an Iberian — And we march through thousand year old English villages. England! England! I'm very happy. Love to you both

RUPERT

This was our last letter from him.

A phrase in it, "bored with the theatre", hurt me; stupidly, of course: but, to top the war's horror, came not merely the danger of the man I loved most — but what seemed a misunderstanding of values. The pain was great; and I wrote back, with a bitterness which hurts today far more than the wound from which it sprang ever hurt: "We are doing some things which matter, if anything does." That letter, written on February 15, reached him, if it did, just before his death.

The unconscious but apparent premonition in these letters of his, form that first light-hearted *ave atque vale!* to the last *England! England! I'm very happy*, is self-evident enough now; the failure to have recognized it, and the potential bitterness closing a friendship like ours — like the quarrel between Deirdre and Naisi on the grave's edge —bring, to the survivor, deep and lonely scrutiny of his own values. All who voluntarily die for a faith answer to the ultimate human test of their cause's credibility, even if it be true that, when they die without glory, their cause's credibility is enhanced. Glory and — it can be said without wronging Brooke—the thrill of new friendships, of fighting for England, and of the isles of Greece, made his death a radiant thing, even for us who looked on. Therefore I like to think that, if he and I could talk today, he would run his fingers through his hair, tweak his nose, grin, and say: "Yes, I'd a fine death, Maurice, but, by God, Edith Cavell had a finer."

A few weeks later, on the evening of May 10, at Columbus, Ohio, Miss Van Volkenburg and I heard that he had died. The news came in a letter which we received just before the curtain rang up on a performance of *The Trojan Women*: we were carrying the play, from coast to coast, in memory of the dead — of all nations — who had died for their faith.

V

THE next production at the Chicago Little Theatre—the opening bill of the 1915-1916 season—was *Lithuania*, presented in conjunction with Andreyev's *Pretty Sabine Women*. The first performance of the play (antedating the English production by several months) took place on October 12, 1915.[32]

The production, which ran three weeks, was a complete failure financially, *Lithuania* proving extremely unpopular. Barker, who saw a performance, disliked it intensely, joining with Marsh's apologetic preference for poems he could read at dinner his own apologetic preference for plays he could see after it; he attributed its unpleasant effect in large part to the manner of its presentation, which he found abominably convincing, and he expressed a peculiar distaste for the Daughter; as this was the effect expressly aimed at by Brooke, who had discussed Miss Van Volkenburg's part with her, and a possible production of the play with me, in some detail, we were all, including Barker, delighted with his tribute.

A small edition of the play, in paper wrappers, with a cover designed by Raymond Jonson, was simultaneously published (at 35 cents) by the Chicago Little Theatre. Through sedulously giving copies away, we succeeded in having only three or four dozen left some two years later, when we raised the price of the remainder to $2.50, at which price, and later at $3.50 and $5.00, they were eagerly bought by the Chicago *cognoscenti* (who today, if they are lucky enough to find a copy, hastily plank down a $20.00 "bill" and scurry off with the treasure-trove in their pocket). At the same time I repurchased from McClurg's and other local book-dealers about thirty copies for the original published price; McClurg's were particularly pleased to get rid of theirs, since they would no longer "accumulate dust and take up valuable space".

Speculation on Brooke's future as a poet, or as a dramatist, can, of course, be only speculation; but he said much to Miss Van Volkenburg and myself which threw light on what he personally held likely. He looked on *Lithuania*, as, for him, a highly significant experiment, partly because his medium compelled him to work within limitations which admitted of no redundancy or elaboration, partly because in it he was concerned with the expression of character, not of personal feeling, and partly because he felt that it was his first important stepping-stone toward tragedy; he recognized that tragedy was the highest of the arts, and hoped that ultimately he might attain to it.

The simplicity, directness, and power of *Lithuania* are strong evidence for believing that his hope would have been fulfilled. The play is an "acting" play from the rise of the curtain to its fall: there is no false or unnecessary word in it; the characters, the situation, the intolerable suspense, the horror of the deed, the reversal, and the appalling climax, are the work of a real dramatist — a dramatist not yet of the first order, it is true, and one who has, perhaps too closely, studied *Macbeth*, but, none the less, of his kind a master-dramatist. For a first play, *Lithuania* is almost unbelievably compelling.[33]

There is no doubt in my own mind that, had Brooke lived, his main work would ultimately have been dramatic. His dominant characteristic was, if I observed him aright, that "gusto" in people and life, which he shared with Keats and Synge: that gusto is the essence of drama; it is not, I think, the essence, though in youth it often takes the form, of lyrical poetry. The *Memoir* shows, and his everyday conversation showed, how large and practical a part the theatre had played in his daily life from boyhood; he had, too, that *nostalgia* of the theatre, which is usually found only in theatrical old-timers, never in the dramatic *dilettante* or the stagestruck. The flippancy of his references to the theatre shows, perhaps more convincingly than anything else to those who knew him best, how seriously he took it. On the other hand, it is obvious that I was a prejudiced observer, and that the very gusto which made him a potential dramatist gave him also the faculty of being "all things to all men".

Perhaps, too, it is significant — though, in view of the letter's recipients, too much stress should not be laid on the point — that, in one of the last letters we had from him, he said: "In the end, those of us who come back will start writing great new plays"; he did not say, "poems". Similarly again I would not stress unduly the fact that, before the war, he, Miss Van Volkenburg, Miss Allenby, and I were planning a close and practical association in theatrical work in Paris, where it was our intention to establish an English theatre in the autumn of 1915; Brooke, like ourselves, was always full of "plans", and the three of us were so happy in our new-found friendship that we inevitably devised schemes which might enable us to stay together. But, while such things must be taken for what they are worth, they are, perhaps, signposts. He had the feeling, which some of us share, that tragedy today prepares to resume her throne, and he sensed a coming rebirth of ritual drama. Perhaps too he showed to us, as to only one other of his friends, and she the closest of them all, a side of himself which he glossed over for most, fearing to be misunderstood. He talked to me, I like to think, as to a poet who had deliberately — in so far as he could — stopped "writing poems" and given himself instead to the theatre with the

hope that, by subordinating literature to drama, he migh
one day learn to help recreating the greatest of the arts

Perhaps that is my vanity: perhaps it is the truth; I d
not know.

VI

ABOUT a year after Brooke's death an envelope came on
day, addressed to me in an unknown handwriting; as
opened it, there dropped out the snapshot printed here: i
was a copy of the photograph taken through a ruse tha
afternoon the *Philadelphia* steamed into Plymouth, by
woman none of us knew. Here, at last, on Miss Van Volker
burg's behalf and my own, she can be thanked. About th
same time I received a letter from Ethel P——, with whon
we had had those happy days on shipboard; in it she said

> I live over so often one night in the saloon of the
> ship. There, where I had already looked, where
> no one new had come, I saw outlined suddenly an
> amazing head. In it life had caught the most
> daring expression of life's loveliness. Well, if for
> a few days Youth walked among us, in its passing
> it left unnumbered years for memory of him who
> gave of it so lavishly. And though the triumphant
> possessor of it has not taken it away, but rather,
> by setting a new star in the sky, leaves it burning
> clear where all who will may see, yet, with the
> adorable human form laid forever aside, I know
> no more than that the pulse of life *does* move

slower. Nor will an hour of vision give it more
than an hour of strength. Life and love and youth,
which overtake, so surely pass.

Brooke, who came honestly by his courage, spoke freely
and often of his mother; in a letter to me a few months after
his death, she said:

> Very soon after war broke out, both my boys
> told me that they must go to fight for their country.
> I agreed at once, and much as I have suffered since,
> I have never regretted it . . . Perhaps you don't know
> that seven weeks after Rupert's death my youngest
> son Alfred was killed in France and now I am quite
> alone . . . One has to go on somehow, though I
> don't know how.

Brooke spoke freely too — in particular, manlike, to
Miss Van Volkenburg — of his love for Miss Allenby.
"Poor Rupert Brooke," the diary-letter says, "carries his
heart in his eyes"; in his girl's presence, the light went out
of him: there was only the lovesick boy. Yet, the tale runs,
there were hours when such a radiance surrounded those
two, that the chance onlooker — recognizing divinity, or,
oftener enough, more likely, appalled by beauty and seeing
the devil in it — averted his eyes: suburban railway-car-
riages, men say, would suddenly empty, and plumbers' wives
run shrieking through Richmond Park. Though I, being
short-sighted with a tendency to astigmatism, never saw
precisely that, yet I perceive the essential truth of the description: myopia, which conceals remoter aspects of the

cosmos, sometimes privileges the spectacled to peer closely into lovers' pores. There are those, however, who maintain that it flattered Miss Allenby to have the handsomest young man in London, and at that the author of *Grantchester*, waiting to pick up her handkerchief; she was not, they claim, the only woman who, before Brooke was born or since he died, had let hers fall. The second half of that statement sounds not improbable: such things, I am told, happen; but over the first there seems to hang a confusing mist, as it were of jealousy. Jealousy loves half-truths. There was no jealousy in an exasperated cry my own well-meaning idiocy once wrung from Miss Allenby herself. We were talking. "Of course you've played the merry devil," said I. "What a masculine phrase," said she; "but I like attracting men, if that's what you mean." "Our folly interests you?" "Folly never interests; if it interests, it isn't folly." "Was Rupert's never folly?" "Oh, how stupid you are! Of course I loved him. And of course he could be as hard as nails."

That hardness was an integral part of him; he would not have been himself without it, just as he would not have been the poet he is, had he never written his "unpleasant" poems. It, and they, came straight out of his young and radiant manhood, tackling "actuality" for all he was worth; it, and they, came straight out of his youth. Youth is not a crime: sometimes it is a triumph; and those who today condemn or pity him for his have forgotten their own: they have forgotten what their own might have been. So, once again, I like to think that, could he and the girl who played the most important part in his sex-life talk tonight, their conversation would run: *He:* "Your babies are adorable: I wish they were mine." *She:* "Hurry up and finish that new play you promised me. And stick to vicarious domesticity."

After his death, "spirit-messages" purporting to come from him were received by some of his acquaintances in America; their burden was always the same: "Courage: adventure: bite deep." "Moon-moping!" a ouija-board once indignantly exclaimed on his behalf to a friend depressed by adversity. That rings true to Brooke. But such things are irrelevant: excellence does not change; experience needs no confirmation. He lived richly; he died bravely; that is enough.

I have tried to write of Brooke, as I knew him, simply, truthfully, without grandiloquence: not "making a story". If there is dishonour in that, the dishonour is not his. My "chatter about Harriet"[34]—Brooke's *bouts-rimés,* straw-hat and the like being, in this case, the offenceless Harriet—has been deliberate: frankly, for all my talk of *Lithuania,* I would sooner have a glimpse of Keats eyeing a little Jewess "with tinkling feet," as she walked down Mile End Road, than know what that other Brown (of Hampstead) thought about the *Ode to a Nightingale.* The man who was Rupert Brooke is written truly in his poems, his letters, and the heart of his friends; when we are dust, posterity will judge him: it will judge him inexorably, and we shall not be there. While I am still here, I would bear my witness. The beauty of the outer man was as the beauty of a young god; the beauty of the inner man outshone the beauty of the outer by so much as the glory of the sun is outshone by the glory of the human heart.

1918-1927

NOTES

NOTES

1. Reprinted, by courteous permission of the editors, from *The Dial* for March, 1918.

2. Undated; *ca.* third week in April, 1914.
   This and the transcripts of the letters, etc., which follow (all, except *The True Beatitude,* holographs), are printed exactly as Brooke wrote them: except that, both in the letters and throughout these *Recollections,* an imaginary name, "Eileen Allenby", has been substituted by me for a real name.

3. He had married my sister.

4. A generous member of the Chicago Little Theatre Association, Mrs. Seymour Edgerton, had, a moment before, given Miss Van Volkenburg and myself two thousand dollars, in order that we might return to Europe that summer and study art-theatres, with particular reference to puppets.

5. Reprinted, by courteous permission of the author, from *An April Elegy,* by Arthur Davison Ficke: Mitchell Kennerley; New York, 1917.

6. A holograph of *The Busy Heart* in Brooke's handwriting on a flyleaf of Miss Van Volkenburg's copy of the *Oxford Book of English Verse* shows several variants in punctuation from the published version, but no important changes.

7. This letter is written in pencil; the paper is torn in several places, the envelope missing, and there is nothing to indicate from what part of New Jersey it was written.

8. For Judge Brack's benefit, it may be explained that this statement belongs to the same category as A World made Safe for Democracy.

9. The painter and stage-decorator, whose work at the Chicago Little Theatre had already begun to win him fame.

10. Mr. Lester Luther, who was playing the part of Lövborg in *Hedda Gabler*.

11. In my reply I had commended him to their care.

12. Mr. Eugene Hutchinson of Chicago.

13. We did; Chicago did not: the Georgian poets had not yet "arrived" . . . in Chicago.

14. Ellen Van Volkenburg became by her marriage a British subject: but not acclimatized.

15. The *Philadelphia* had been converted from a three-class into a two-class boat.

16. Next to us was sitting Ronald Hargreave, the painter, and the four of us had instantaneously foregathered.

17. We later came to know him, a charming and widely-travelled man and again a distinguished painter.

18. M. B.

19. The English folk-singer, one of the "Fuller Sisters" of adorable memory.

20. First published in Mr. Marsh's *Memoir*, and reprinted by his courteous permission. The *ms.* from which the above version is taken was copied by me, at the time of the sonnet's composition, from the original holograph; it shows the following variants from that published by Mr. Marsh:

Original Version   *Version published in the Memoir*

1.2. *Last Curtain* .... *last curtain*

  3. *Puppets have* .... *Mimes will have*

  4. *God, worship and love and sing,*.. *Author, worship love and sing;*

        (Was not a comma intended here after *worship*?)

Original Version	Version published in the Memoir
5.	The two commas omitted
6. *some*	*a*
10.	Dash omitted
12. *divines*	*divine*

There is also a slight variation in the indentation of the sestet.

These variants (otherwise of no more importance than the sonnet itself) show that Brooke took the latter seriously enough to work on it afterwards.—The second sonnet, too, has been "doctored" by its author, with more reason and less excuse.—The punning references in the 12th and 13th lines of both sonnets are to the priests at our table, who looked with not entire approval on our daily levity.

21. The original *ms.* of this masterpiece was enclosed in the diary-letter. The 1st, 4th, 7th, and 10th lines were by Brooke and are in his handwriting; the 2nd, 5th, 8th and 11th were by Miss Van Volkenburg, the 3rd, 6th, 9th and 12th by me. The rest of these otherwise immortal poems—there must have been a dozen or more—died (fortunately) at birth.

22. Reference to the ballad will show the palpable injustice of this charge: the two other co-authors were plainly referring to an anonymous lady in the dining-saloon.

23. Miss Van Volkenburg had been ill before leaving America.

24. This verse, together with the title and date, was written by Brooke in the diary-letter.

25. See note 8.

26. The variation in spelling is Brooke's.

27. We had planned in Birmingham to have lunch with him on Thursday and to leave for the Continent the same afternoon.

28. *Lithuania*; we received a copy shortly afterwards, corrected and autographed by Brooke. It is now in the possession of Mr. Alexander Greene, of Chicago.

29. Miss Harriet Monroe, editor of *Poetry*.
30. "This...too crude stuff" was the *1914* sonnets, which were enclosed. They are now in the possession of Miss Monroe.
31. *New Numbers*.
32. The cast was as follows:

A Stranger	Edward Moseman
The Mother	Miriam Kiper
The Daughter	Ellen Van Volkenburg
The Father	Maurice Browne
A Young Man	George Wolff
The Vodka-Shopkeeper	Louis Alter
The Vodka-Shopkeeper's Son	Allan Ross McDougall

The play was staged by Raymond Jonson and directed by me.
33. In a manual entitled *The Craftsmanship of the One-Act Play* (Little, Brown and Company, 1923), its author, a Mr. Percival Wilde, says of *Lithuania*: "I have always doubted its authorship"; he gives as his reason the stage-directions' "Teutonic English . . . of which Rupert Brooke, even in his immature days, seems to me to have been incapable."

Mr. Wilde further informs us that "Paul is a young man who has nothing whatever to do with the play . . . A more hopeless development cannot well be conceived. The scene with (him) is entirely unnecessary and distinctly injurious. The action . . . decreases continually in interest." It would appear that Mr. Wilde does not think much of *Lithuania*. It would also appear that the value of his critical faculty in questioning its authenticity measures the value of his critical faculty in expurgating Paul: Mr. Wilde, in common with many of his profession, has a charming sexual naiveté.
34. The reference is not to *Poetry's* blameless editor.

Hotel McAlpin

Greeley Square

New York City

MERRY & BOOMER,
MANAGERS.

May 24.
1914.

Dear Mr. Hutchinson,

Modern photographers seem to an old-fashioned person like me, to retouch almost _too_ much. Or perhaps you only take the soul? The soul of persons who write verse is said to be hermaphroditic, but not, I protest, so feminine.

Poor lady, she is on her way back again.

Yours sincerely
Rupert Brooke

ELLEN VAN VOLKENBURG AS THE DAUGHTER IN "LITHUANIA."

DEMOCRACY AND THE ARTS

DEMOCRACY
AND THE ARTS

_____

Rupert Brooke

WITH A PREFACE BY
GEOFFREY KEYNES

PREFACE

RUPERT BROOKE went up to King's College, Cambridge, as an undergraduate in October, 1906. The political influences of his home life at Rugby had been strongly Liberal, but soon after arriving at Cambridge he began to show a tendency to move towards the Left. An early friend at King's was Hugh Dalton, now Chancellor of the Exchequer in the Labour Government. Dalton was then Honorary Secretary of the Cambridge University Fabian Society, and he has recorded [1] that in April, 1907, Brooke came to him and said, "I'm not your sort of Socialist; I'm a William Morris sort of Socialist, but I want to join your Society as an Associate". According to Dalton, he soon saw the intellectual limitations of a "William Morris sort of Socialist" and then became a full member of the Fabian Society. For the academic year 1909–1910 he was elected President. Meetings were sometimes held in Brooke's rooms in King's, where, as J. T. Sheppard, now Provost of the College, recalls, the Fabians would be entertained to a frugal repast of bread and cheese and beer. At these meetings he was never tired of teaching the importance of poets and artists in the good society of the future, and Dalton has also testified that " he came to talk very good sense on the larger economic questions".

It was probably during his Presidency of the

[1] In the *Memoir* by Sir Edward Marsh first published with the *Collected Poems* in 1918.

C.U.F.S., in the spring or summer of 1910, that Brooke read his paper to the Fabians entitled "Democracy and the Arts". I was myself present at the meeting as an Associate Member, though I cannot now remember any details of the occasion. I fear that I had joined the Society rather to please my friend than because of any deep political convictions, but I felt rewarded by having the stimulus and enjoyment of listening to speakers such as Bernard Shaw and, on more than one occasion, Brooke himself. The meeting is likely to have been in Brooke's rooms in Gibb's Buildings in the south-west corner of the first court of King's, and the speaker must have looked exactly as he appears in the portrait-study reproduced here from a photograph taken in 1910 by a Fellow of Trinity, V. H. Mottram.[1] Brooke was very much in earnest over his Socialism at this time, and even more in earnest in his solicitude for the Arts, particularly the art of poetry. By 1910 he had already been taking himself seriously as a poet for six or seven years, and his first volume of poetry was to appear in the next year, 1911. But in the early part of 1910 the endowment of Artists by a Socialist Government must have seemed a remote Utopian ideal, important indeed while engaging our attention through the vivid personality of our President, but only to be quickly forgotten when the evening's discussion was over with the disappearance of the bread and cheese and beer.

A few years after Brooke's death in 1915 his

[1] Late Professor of Physiology in the University of London.

PREFACE

mother gave me the manuscript of "Democracy and the Arts" during one of my periodical visits to her house at Rugby, and for nearly twenty-five years it has lain more or less unregarded in my library. Now, in 1946, the subject of the paper has suddenly become topical, more topical than when it was written, with the dawning of the Socialist State in England of which Brooke was one of the Minor Prophets. It has, therefore, seemed to me to be my duty [1] to present his paper for publication in print, since the claims of the Arts can so easily be overlooked among the many more material and pressing problems. Were he still alive, none would now be more eager to serve the Arts than Rupert Brooke, and it is therefore right to allow his voice, which will still be heard with respect, to speak to a wider public than the long-vanished gathering of young intellectuals who listened to him in his college rooms.

But his reputation as a poet and a writer must not arouse expectations of a polished literary composition in the pages that follow. It is obvious from the appearance of the pencilled manuscript that it was dashed off at a great speed, and it was read with but little revision. It is brusque and colloquial in style, with none of the literary graces of which the writer was capable. It was meant to be an example of what the Poet could do when he turned practical, and its value lies in the sincerity of the convictions which informed his mind, and the urgency with which he

[1] With the concurrence of Brooke's other Literary Trustees, Walter de la Mare, the Provost of King's and Dudley Ward.

could present his case even when there was no immediate prospect of a system of society likely to be
willing to carry it into effect. Even under a Coalition
Government, and in conditions of war, a beginning
was made in the recognition of the Arts by the
official institution of C.E.M.A., now known as The
Arts Council. Perhaps Brooke's words will remind
the present Chancellor of the Exchequer (who may,
indeed, never have forgotten) that once he too
believed in the importance of the Arts in the national
life, and he may be encouraged to assign to this
object the funds that could do so much, if applied in
the right way, to encourage the artists and to foster
appreciation of their arts.

GEOFFREY KEYNES

May, 1946

DEMOCRACY AND THE ARTS

I AM NOT going to rhapsodize about the Spirit of Democracy as dawning in the operas of Wagner or the anarchic prose of Whitman or Carpenter. "Brotherhood" will not be heard of in this paper. Neither comrade nor cumrade shall be mentioned by me. I would detain you this side of the millennium. What I want to discuss, to ask one or two questions about, is the effect that a democratic form of society—*our* democratic form of society—has, and will have, on the production of pictures, music and literature; and how we are to control that effect. I nearly wrote a paper on "The Artist under Socialism", but I didn't for two reasons. One was that the phrase "under Socialism" regrettably tends to drop the pink gauze of unreality over the whole issue. The other was that I wanted not to scare off any good people, who, though Progressive, Democratic, Socialistic and the rest, can't bring themselves to be so absolutely sure as to call themselves *Socialists*, [or to believe] that the pearl-button industry really *ought* to be taken over by the State—at any rate just *yet*.

I use the word "Democracy". It seems to me that this century is going to witness a struggle between Democracy and Plutocracy. Democracy is the ordering of the national life according to the national will. Its probable and desirable increase in the near future entails a great growth in collective control, in various ways, of every side of the life of the nation, and

organizing—or wilfully not organizing—it to attain
the collectively-willed good. It is not the time now to
spread into how this growth of Democracy will insist
on a great liberty and security and independence for
each man. I feel sure that in this general question most
people, in theory anyhow, will agree with me. And
in the end it is one of the few questions that matter. I
am one of those who care for the *result* of actions. If
anybody tells me that an absolute hereditary mon-
archy based on slave labour, or an agricultural oli-
garchy of Plato's φύλακες, is the ideal state which *he*
will always advocate, I can only take him up to a high
place, and say, "My dear creature, up North there are
twenty millions who want Democracy; down South
there are twenty millions who want Plutocracy. Are
you coming North with me?" And the same to any
Democrat who tries to differ with me about, say, the
exact relations between Local and National Government fifty years on.

This democratization of our land, then, which we
so greatly desire (and which will require, I believe, so
much Collectivism), will reduce the number of those
who live on money they do not earn most or all their
lives. Observe the situation, and remember it's a real
one, not one in a book. (1) Art is important. (2) The
people who produce art at present are, if you look
into it, nearly always dependent on unearned income.
(3) We are going to diminish and extinguish the
number of those dependent on unearned income. We
shall also reduce the number of those rich enough
to act the patron to artists, and change in a thousand

other ways the circumstances of the arts and of the artists.

We must, then, acknowledge that there may be something in the objections of the average anti-democrat, the refined vague upper-class person, that we are making the arts impossible. The literature of the future will be blue-books, its art framed plans of garden cities. The anti-democrat himself is generally easy enough to answer. The decay of Culture, he wails, the neglect of Art, the absence of fine literature —points to the halfpenny papers, shudders at the grimy Philistines. You ask him how often *he* goes to the National Gallery, how lately *he* has read the six best plays of Shakespeare. . . . But the fact remains. Very little attention is paid, as we change the structure of Society, to the claims of the Arts. Artists have lived, in the past and present, on inherited capital or on the patronage of rich men or corporations. How are *we* going to arrange for them? I sympathize —slightly—with those who airily cry, with Whistler, "Art? Oh, Art—*happens!*" But that won't do. It never would, or should, have done. Now least of all. For while everything has, in a way, "happened" hitherto, *now* we are trying this tremendous experiment of Democracy, of taking our own fate into our own hands, controlling the future, shaping Life to our will. Now most of all when we are, however roughly, trying to foresee and provide for everything, we must provide for Art. It is permissible to take what flowers you find best in a wood. A garden requires planning.

I've indicated what I mean by Democracy. I suppose the Arts don't need definition. Both these things will become clearer in the course of the paper. We want to see how we can produce as large and appreciative a public as possible; a state of things where the fineness (not the refinedness) of Art will enter deeply into many men's lives, and as many good works of art as possible. It is this last thing I am most concerned with, dealing with the producers and production, not the questions of distribution or consumption.

But it may be useful to discuss what we mean by Art a little further. The air is full of sentimentalities and false notions about it, and should be cleared. A good many people—especially democratic people—will say the question of Art and Artists has already been answered, and point to William Morris and the Arts and Crafts. This is very dangerous. There are several perils connected with that sort of thing. No answer to the question of Artists has come from these sources; not even a realization of the question. I want to disavow almost altogether what Mr. H. G. Wells once called Hampstead-and-Hammered-Copper Socialism (that was before he went to live at Hampstead). For one thing you must separate the questions of Art and of Crafts. *Crafts* I won't discuss now, beyond suggesting that you can't get a revival of Crafts by any movement consisting of people making a piece of unpolished furniture a year and living on dividends, and of bookbinding by unoccupied young ladies. It must come, if at all, through the Trades Unions. And anyhow, don't mix up Art and Crafts.

It is so easy to do so, and so tempting to slide from
the keen edge of Art into the byways, the pursuits
that don't disturb, the paths that lead to antiquarian-
ism and hobbies, bibliography, love of seventeenth-
century prose which is quaint, beautiful handwriting.
These things are excellent, but not to the point.
Revive handicrafts as much as you can for the sake
of the Craftsman. Art is a different matter. We want
King Lear and " The Polish Rider " for what we get
out of them, not the pleasure it gives Shakespeare and
Rembrandt to make them. Morris, or at least the
Morrisite, approaches the matter from a wrong side.
It is no good going back to the Middle Ages and the
great communal art of the Cathedrals and the folk-
songs. If you can revive communal art, well and good.
But it is a small thing. We have done much better
since. Individuals have made tunes and poems as good
as those we are told came from the people. Burns,
perhaps, has done so. And you won't find any band
of mediæval rustics in an inn inspired to troll out
Paradise Lost or a Beethoven Concerto between the
bouts of mead.

We live in our own age (a very intelligent and
vital one) and we must throw ourselves in with all
its arts and schools of art, music, and literature.
Tapestries are both unhealthy and ugly. Let romaunt
and clavicithern moulder together.

But there arises from *dicta* of Morris a belief that
too many hold—that art is an easy thing, a πάρεργον.
Morris said, I believe, that all poetry ought to be of
the kind a man can make up while he is working at

a loom. Much of his own was. That may be why a lot of it is so dull. "Easy writing", someone said, "makes damned hard reading". Not so did Shakespeare or Balzac write or Beethoven compose. It is an infamous heresy of his, and it extends to other arts besides poetry, though it is about poetry most people hold it. It leads to this too common idea that the various artists of the future will be able to do ordinary work for so many hours a day, and pursue their arts in their leisure time. You don't find artists advocating that: only some of the ordinary cultured public. It is a thing we can't allow. It means the death of the Arts, a civilization of amiable amateurs, of intermittent Alexandrians. We have too much of this system already—it is no fault of the individual—the Civil Service poets, the stockbroker who does watercolours in the evenings, the music-master who has the holidays to compose in. Better, almost, a literature of blue-books than a literature of belles-lettres.

There is another wrong notion of art that falsifies the opinions of many on this subject. Let us beware of those who talk of "the art of the people", or of "expressing the soul of the Community". The Community hasn't got a soul; you can't voice the soul of the Community any more than you can blow its nose. The conditions of Democracy may profoundly alter the outlook of many artists, and partly their style and subject matter. But the *main* business of art has been, is, and, one must assume, will be an individual and unique affair. "I saw—*I* saw", the artist says, "a tree against the sky, or a blank wall in the sunlight, and it was so thrilling, so arresting, so particularly itself, that—well really, I *must* show you! . . . There!" Or the writer explains, "Just so and just so it happened, or might happen, and thus the heart shook, and thus . . ." And suddenly, deliciously, with them you see and feel.

Art is not a criticism of Life. There *is* a side of it that makes problems clear, throws light on the complexity of modern life, assists one to understand. It is a function much dwelt on nowadays. A section of modern drama is praised for explaining religion, or the relation of the sexes, or of Capital and Labour. It is incidental. Discussion is merely one of the means, not the end, of literary art. You are in the midst of insoluble problems of temperance reform and education and organization. The artist, as artist, is not concerned. He leads you away by the hand and, Mamillius-like, begins his tale: "There was a man—dwelt by a churchyard"—it is purely irrelevant.

But how important these intimate irrelevances are! I hold the view most fervently. If not this paper would be found inexcusable—quite inexcusable. Yet I must apologize to those who hold it a waste of time to consider anything for the moment but material social reform. With all my soul I'm with them. I feel deeply with Morris when he cries out about "filling up this terrible gap between riches and poverty. Doubtless many things will go to filling it up, and if Art must be one of those things, let it go. (What business have we with Art at all unless we can share it?) I am not afraid but that Art will rise from the Dead, whatever else lies there". And if it were a choice between keeping the Arts and establishing a high National Minimum, I would not hesitate a moment. I hate the *dilettante* and unimaginative hypocrisy that would. But things don't happen that way. We have forsworn Revolution for a jog-trot along Social Reform, and there is plenty of time to take things with us on the way—Art above all. The tradition of art-work and artists is worth keeping—the sort of tradition, I mean, that links Milton and Keats and Francis Thompson. It is a jumping ground, not a clog. The heritage is valuable. Art, if it cannot make men much better as means, can make them very good as ends. To most people it can give something. To some it can give the highest and supremest part of their lives. It multiplies the value of the life we are trying to organize to have. Not only for the moments when we hear or read or see the Arts do we prize them, though these would be hard to know the full worth of. But when the tree or the wall or the situation meets us in real life, they find profounder hosts. In the transience and hurry Art opens out every way on to the Eternal Ends.

*   *   *   *   *

Democracy and the Arts! This paper, like all good papers, has given its first half to saying what it's going to be about. Like all good papers it had better give most of its second half to saying why it is about it.

Partly because, as I have said, we are on the way to extinguish artists by destroying the systems which enabled them to live. Only the most fanatical and the most immediately popular could survive—by no means the best types. But in any case other systems have been irregular and bad—most of all the present one. We can do something far better. Also, we *must* realize that in a thousand ways new conditions and vast possibilities are round us and ahead. The circumstances of modern life offer new temptations and new dangers to the artist. Enormous potential art publics grow slowly before our eyes. And both they and the artist are increasingly helpless before the blind amoral profit-hunger of the commercial. We must not be unprepared for the effects these dark multitudes will have on the Arts.

The question of the Public of the future requires consideration, though it is not the central point of this paper. We want it large and varied. A culture sustained by an infinitesimal group of the infinitely elect will not be possible or desirable. Though, indeed, there are, and increasingly will be, many groups each thinking itself to be such: and a good thing too, so long as the conditions of modern life keep the groups from getting too isolated and stagnant. We need not complain if the Public only means a mass of little publics. It would be a good thing if the whole artistic public of England twenty years hence would delight in Gauguin. We shall be content if half a million worship the Impressionists, and half a million adore the Post-Impressionists. It may be one of the conditions of life. It is especially one of the things we must fearlessly accustom ourselves to, the growth of diverse circles and publics, to whom local or special kinds of poets and painters will appeal. From such artists the greater, and more widely reaching, will roughly emerge, spreading to other circles, more distant ears and eyes. It used to be, in a general way, true to say of a great author—of Dryden or Johnson or Pope—that all England read them—all England that read any literature. That time has utterly gone—it is not realized how irrevocably that time has gone. There are twenty millions who read in England today, millions of them reading literature. The numbers of a potential literary public increase enormously year by year. No one man, except one or two classics, can touch more than a fraction. This change in the old conditions, this breaking up of unity, this multitude of opening minds, may bring perplexity and apparent confusion of standards; but also (I say it soberly) the chance of vast, unimaginable, unceasing additions to the glory of the literature of England.

There are two other points, points on which many go wrong when they contemplate the present and future publics for the Arts. There is the mistake of the man who says, "When Everyman has reached a decent amount of leisure and education, the whole community will foster and patronize and delight in the Arts". An inspection of the class that has had leisure and education does not justify this opinion. It may be objected that public school education is not good. That is true. But it will be a long time before you can ensure the whole nation getting a considerably better education than the modern public school and university one. And even then I do not suppose more than a small part of the nation will ever be much interested in the Arts, though it is easy to imagine a state of things coming to pass where perhaps most people will pretend to be. But such things are beyond our vista. The first generation of universal education has not given us a nation of art-lovers. Nor will the second, nor the third. We must face the problem on the assumption that public demand isn't going to settle much of it for us for a long while yet.

And then there's the idea that the lower classes, the people who are entering into the circle of the educated, are coarsely devoid of taste, likely to swamp—swamping—the whole of culture in undistinguished, raucous, stumpy arts that know no tradition. If the washy, dull, dead upper-class brains this idea haunts were its only home we could leave it. But it lurks in the Victorian shadows and dusty corners of finer types of mind. Ideas in other parts of this paper may help to kill it, I hope. I would say one or two things about it here. In the first place, it is not relevant that the newly encivilized and educated classes should not be able to leap at once to the superb heights to which we have toiled through so many generations. It is the future—their future fineness—we work for. It is only natural that the taste of the lower classes should be at present infinitely worse than ours. The amazing thing is that it is probably rather better. It is true many Trades Unionists do not read

Milton. Nor do many University men. But take the best of each. Compare the literary criticism of the *Labour Leader* with that of the *Saturday Review*. It is, I assure you, enormously better, enormously readier to recognize good new literature. Think of the working-class support of Miss Horniman's Repertory Theatre in Manchester. Compare the fate of the progeny of middle- and upper-class intellectualism, Mr. Frohman's Repertory Theatre, and the Vedrenne-Barker company, and Mr. Herbert Trench's dream. Compare the style of the *Cambridge History of English Literature* with that of Mr. Arnold Bennett's handbook on the subject. They are separated—how can I express the difference?—more widely than Hell and Heaven. The gulf that parts them is the greatest gulf there is, the one which divides the dead from the living. Put, finally—for we must stop this sometime—put the *Spectator* beside the *Clarion* for pure literary merit. I do not wish to decry the *Spectator*. In common with many other Socialists I have written in it. But—on the honour of an enthusiast for literature—the *Clarion* wins all the way. Those who have determined to make the State we live in, and are forming for the future, as fine as possible, must be very careful to oppose the force of primness in this matter. Unnecessarily to divide the traditions we have got from the new life of the time, to assist in divorcing good taste from popular literature, is to rob and weaken both. Those whose test of painting is perspective, whose test of literature is the absence of split infinitives, cry

"Vulgarity!" and "Bad Grammar!" They are the epithets corpses fling at the quick, dead languages at living. Accept them and pass on. They do not matter. More, they are praise.

I have met a group of young poets in London. Some of them are in money extremely poor. They talk Cockney. And they write—some are good, others bad—as they talk. That is to say, their poems give fullest value when pronounced as they thought and felt them. They allow for *ow* being *aow*. Their love-poems begin (I invent) "If yew wd come agin to me". That is healthy. That way is life. In them is more hope—and more fulfilment—than in the old-world passion and mellifluous despair of any gentleman's or lady's poetry.

To sum up, the influence of Democracy on the Arts from this point of view—the Public—need not be bad. To show that it is good, and to make it better, it is most importantly our duty to welcome and aid all the new and wider movements that come with the growth of Democracy and the rise of new generations. I say new generations, for we are old-fashioned I find, in danger of being out of touch, we whose life is divided between university, a few similar people in London, and the country rectories that are our homes. And it is even more important when we see the idols we most worship attacked and crumbling, to acquiesce, to accept where we cannot understand, to endure the boots and accent of the unrefined in the sanctuary, for the sake of the new Gods that follow. It will be very difficult.

But the subject I am most concerned with now is, as I said at the beginning, that of the Artist himself, how we are to make certain of his turning up. It would be more amusing than profitable to go into the economic status of the Artist in past times, a study that has not been sufficiently worked out. At least notice that no past age can jeer at us and go unscathed. Take literature. To each generation of the last century we can reply with John Clare and James Thomson and Francis Thompson. Ask those of the great age of letters, the eighteenth century, what they did with Chatterton, who might have been the greatest of them all. Consider Michael Drayton, and a dozen more of the Elizabethans. The truth is that no system has worked well for long. With painters I believe the guild system did for a time. The State in Athens, founded, we are told, on popular good taste, out-rivalled the great courts of Syracuse and elsewhere. Our problems are different from theirs; our machinery cannot be so simple. Patronage is often loosely praised, held up to us as the golden age for artists. It is grossly over-estimated. Once or twice it has worked: Italy will witness. And the conception of musicians, poets and painters, healthy and wealthy, crowding round a prince of perfect taste, perfect appearance, and immense generosity, is delightful. But who will honestly hope our millionaires will fill their distinguished places? And it was an untrust-worthy transient business. It only works with a small rich court of highly cultured people. Patronage, to be of great use, must endow the artist thoroughly.

The ordinary system of incomplete endowment and jobbery and such things as payment for dedications, was a ramshackle affair. You see it at work in Elizabethan times, when most of the best writers lost all their shame (which doesn't much matter) and half their vitality (which does) in cadging and touting. They were in continual poverty and debt, and driven to hackwork. Few dramatists could make as much as the equivalent of £200 a year. Jobbing was all right when it could be invoked and if it jobbed the man into a sinecure. Often, as with Spenser, it didn't. So we have lost half the *Faery Queen* (oh, *I* shouldn't care if we'd lost it all. It's the principle of the thing). It has been the same since. It is impossible to know how much more Milton and Marvell would have given us if they had had money enough to live on. If anything at all, the loss is enormous. If Dryden and Addison had not had to sell themselves to politics, our literature could only have gained.

Only in a few cases and in a few kinds of literature have writers been able to make a living. Even lately and with the most popular this is true. Tennyson did not make enough to live on till he was middle-aged. He had to put off his marriage eleven years. Tom Hood, a great writer, both comic and serious, was, artistically, ruined by the continuous flood of jokes he had to pour forth all his life. And, in the waste of the past centuries, you must not only count the cases of starvation or over-production, nor even the artistic potentialities sown here and there in the undistinguished mass of the people, which have perished unconscious in that blindest oblivion—the mute inglorious Miltons of the village and slum Beethovens—but also the many who have had the chance of an artist's career that would have produced good, and have not thought the risk worth while. Alfred Tennyson died, but was not born, the only poet in that family.

And nowadays: it is worth considering what we do, or rather what Fate does, now, to enable artists to produce works of art. It is terrifying, when you examine the matter, to find how many of them live on unearned, presumably inherited, capital. As there are comparatively few people who can do this, a million or two, and as we are going to reduce the number, it is an alarming outlook. The only creative artistic profession you have much chance of making a living at, fairly soon, is that of a dramatist. I suppose it is almost inconceivable that a creative musician can live by composing till he has passed thirty; few then. It is in the process of making a public that the modern artist has to have extraneous financial support or go under. (There are various ways of going under. Mr. Somerset Maugham and Mr. Hall Caine chose one way, the better. Rimbaud, who went East and was last heard of driving a caravan in Arabia,[1] another. Chatterton a third.) The painter's only hope is to paint the portraits of the extremely rich and extremely undistinguished. It is not always

[1] Brooke is here at fault. Rimbaud, after travelling in Abyssinia, died in hospital at Marseilles.

open, nor always attractive, to him to take the revenge Sargent sometimes takes. In future, perhaps, we'll have our big painters painting the great, not the rich.

Poetry is even worse off than the other arts. Even Mr. Rudyard Kipling could not live on his poetry. Very few poets, perhaps one or two in five years, sell 1000 copies of a volume. If they do, and if they find a very generous publisher, and if they charge 5s. for their volume (an absurdly high price) they get £25! An experienced publisher's reader tells me no one in England makes £50 a year by poetry—except perhaps Mr. Kipling and Mr. A. Noyes. Fiction's far better: but you can't live by writing good fiction —so writers of good fiction inform me. Henry James can *now*, no doubt, at sixty. He could not if he were thirty.

What then, as we grow more democratic and more people have to work for their living, since the noblest work of all does not produce a livelihood, are we to do? To make a great creative artist is beyond the power of eugenist or schoolmaster. All we can hope to do is to spot them when they come, and enable them to realize their genius. We have laid down one axiom—the artist is to be free from other work. If you won't do that, at any rate let the other work be as disgusting as possible. An artist will do better art-work in intervals if his livelihood is got by cleaning sewers than if he takes up some more fascinating occupation, like teaching or critical work. But if we're going to do away with the very clumsy and inefficient machinery of patrons (who don't work at all now) and inherited capital, we, the community, must endow the artist. This has often enough been put forward as a necessary part of some Utopian—probably strongly Collectivist—State, the sort of State the year 2050 may see. I submit that it is a thing that should be begun now. It should go on concurrently with taxation; be a financially minor, but actually important, part of the annual Budget. It is absurd to wait till the Death Duties have done their work, to begin remedying the bad effects of it. With scholarships, of course, a little is done this way; but very little and very clumsily and very unconsciously. This evening I want to suggest a few ideas about endowment. If people accept the general theory, a detailed plan would not be hard to elaborate. It is the sort of idea that must be accepted generally as commonsense, not a startling novelty, and must be part of the ordinary background of people's minds. Fix your eye firmly on what we want to do, to endow the great creative artists. Now it must obviously be endowment for ever. It is no use paying a man to learn the intricacies of musical composition for seven or eight years and then leaving him stranded. It is just the greatest who would suffer. Verdi might come out of it all right: not Wagner. Nor can we have anyone dictating to the artists how they must work, on pain of having their scholarships taken away. A system so brilliantly efficacious with undergraduates and schoolboys would not work in this case. Nor, of course, could questions of morality enter. And the endowment must not be removed if the artist becomes popular enough to earn a living without it. We don't want to prolong the present condition by which, if an artist strikes a vein which is popular, he is economically bound to continue in it for the rest of his life. By that, Shakespeare, being successful with histories, daren't proceed to *As You Like It*, or, having "scored a success" in comedy, can't go on to *Hamlet*. No, the endowment must be unconditioned, even, I suggest, as regards production. We might perhaps insist on one picture, book, or piece of music in ten years. Nothing more stringent. The only debatable point seems to me to be the forbidding of other trades. We *might* forbid them to earn money by doing quite different work to any large extent. No doubt the Government will begin that way. I expect it's not worth doing, though. There are a lot of details, like the increase of endowment if the artist married. The Eugenics Society would see we got that.

The point where most people profess to find the greatest difficulty is in the machinery for selecting people for endowment. "The State", they say, "is always stupid about Art". Also "a Committee always compromises". They talk of "officialdom". As every Socialist knows, these silly generalizations are always being flung in to cloak muddled thinking. To begin with, the State hasn't tried anything of this kind. It has only muddled feebly with Art here and there. To argue from that is like bringing up the bad management of occasional railways by individualist governments as an argument against the considered socialization of monopolies. In any case, State activity is not uniformly stupid. The Royal Academy perhaps is bad. The National Gallery is good. So, on the whole, is the Civil List—as far as it goes. The chief faults in these two departments are those of meanness. We can remedy that if we want to.

As far as efficiency of endowment goes, any modern Cabinet Minister with a few hundred thousand a year to spend and the advice of a couple of literary journalists would be more successful, and infinitely less wasteful, than the present system of capital. But that is a low standard. And the one-man method is not the best. A committee is obvious. It is a system that fulfills its purpose very well, for example, in electing to college fellowships, especially where the number of fellowships is large. For notice, the ordinary objections to a committee on an æsthetic subject apply only when it is to choose some single object. A committee of artists met to select one from one thousand designs, say for a bridge across the Thames, will compromise and not choose the most beautiful. But if the Supreme and Omniscient Art Critic required them to pick the ten most beautiful, and gave them one hundred shots, they would probably succeed. And that is what we want. Take the endowment of pure creative literature. I conceive of a committee of, say, thirty. It could and should be constituted in many different ways, by nomination by the Crown, by, perhaps, the Universities, by various official and semi-official bodies such as the

Society of Authors, and in other ways—the more irregular the better. You'd get a few stuffy people, no doubt; you'd also get a few creative artists, Thomas Hardy and Yeats, and critics like Professor Sir Walter Raleigh and Mr. Gosse. They would have outer circles of advisers and suggesters. It seems to me certain that, if such a Committee had to choose one hundred writers of poetry to endow, and voted on some system of proportional representation, in such a way that two or three, or even one, who was keen enough, could make certain of a candidate, they would sweep in almost every writer who could possibly turn out to be any good. Remember, it is people like these who have always been the first to recognize genius. Think how Tennyson or James Thomson or Yeats or Meredith were discovered. Think, from the other side, of the work Henley and Ben Jonson did.

It may be objected that we should waste a lot in endowing failures, ten of them perhaps for every one even moderate success. Certainly. It is an integral part of the scheme. The choice is between endowing twenty Tuppers to one Byron—and endowing neither; and the present system, which consists in endowing twenty thousand Tuppers and one Byron, *and*—for that might be worth while—very effectually disendowing and spoiling twenty million Tuppers—and who dare say how many Byrons among them?

Indeed, I'd have you notice that the kind of failures we endow are likely to be useful to our purpose. There is frequently among artists of all kinds generosity that seems extraordinary in a commercial age. The example of French painters is a notable one. And there are several cases today in literature, where good writers of some genius have been helped with money, advice and advertisement, most freely and solely for their genius' sake, by smaller writers of more fortunate lot—just the kind who would have been endowed on their early promise, and would not have accomplished anything great.

That is all to the good. For we must insist on the need for as many channels as possible through which the Arts may be subsidized. Each additional channel may mean fresh artists who would have escaped our notice otherwise; and each helps to provide for fresh, unexpected developments.

Besides the central State endowments it would be a good thing to have more local and special ones. If the numerous universities of Great Britain could be given money to endow creative artistic work, it would be excellent. At present they only endow critical work and knowledge. They would be able to do the other, too, quite admirably. Municipalities also might be encouraged to take steps in that direction. The more progressive of them are ready enough to be the first, driven by those motives of honourable rivalry which already have so finely influenced some of our great cities and districts. With the present growth of local pride, and of universities in large centres, and with the system of County Council scholarships, it should be easy to encourage local endowment of Art, with desirable results of variety and thoroughness. I can imagine Manchester and others being keen enough to get the credit of connexion with the next great painter or dramatist.

This local connexion may be increased and improved incidentally by a plan that has been suggested, by which the local or national authority endowing might receive, under conditions, a share in, or the whole of, the copyright of an endowed artist's work after his death. This applies only, apparently, to music and books. But the lines on which it may be extended to pictures can be seen if you consider the admirable proposal that a percentage of the *increase* in value of a picture should go to the artist or his heirs every time it is sold. This copyright business may allay the fears of the parsimonious, for obviously the State would begin to *gain* by the endowment of Art in a generation. Still it is very important. The cost of endowing Art in England is absurdly small. Suppose you give artists an average of £500 a year—and I personally think *half* that is all that is necessary. Endow for life two hundred musicians, two hundred painters and sculptors, two hundred poets, and three hundred other creative literary men, keeping one hundred endowments for special richness in one section or unclassified creative artistic genius, you would spend half a million a year. Half a million! I need not tell students of modern budgets what a drop that is. If anyone wants to realize its insignificance let him consider modern expenditure on armaments. Half a million to secure the Arts in England! (I appeal to my friends the

politicians in this Society to see that this is done!)
If there's any politician present there's his chance!

* * * * *

Each Art has different conditions and demands
different treatment. I am afraid I have considered too
much the conditions of Literature. But the principles
of endowment apply throughout in music and painting. The system of scholarships from County Council
and other schools is good enough, but must be
continually increased. We want to drain the nation.
More scholarships should come both through the
County Councils and at the various Academies and
Colleges of Music and Art, which, conditionally,
could be State-aided. They must be sufficient in
amount and period. People should be able to travel
and study on them.

(If anyone wants to know how well, even now,
such scholarships can be applied, he can examine
the L.C.C. Art scholarships. To be sure they don't
lead to dead Official Art, ask anyone at the Slade
School of Art, which is not generally thought to be
over-academic. He will tell you of the extraordinarily
good scholars they get from the L.C.C. You will
learn of the Michael Angelo of the twentieth century,
as a youth is named who has been discovered in the
back streets of London, and can draw better than any
upper-class rival. It is the right process. I'm told by
people at the Slade that the holders of L.C.C. scholarships are some of the best people there. And that

they should be sent or be able to go to the Slade
shows that these municipal bodies wouldn't encourage only dead official art.)

I will not worry about more details. I only want to
insist that endowment is the only thing for us to do,
and is immediately necessary. In considering such a
scheme certain requirements must be kept in mind as
a guide. The artist must be able to devote himself to
his work. He must be left to himself as much as
possible. He should have, I think, an economic spur
to production and popularity, the chance, that is, of
greater wealth if his work catches on. And endowment should be of as various kinds as possible.

And besides all these more or less official forces at
work, we must see that there are private ones. More
and more as the public for the Arts grows wider shall
we find private societies and groups in immense
variety helping our work. This may take the form of
endowment, group-patronage, an excellent thing,
already less rare than is generally known. It requires
a genuine and rather beautiful faith in an artist's
work and future for large numbers of his friends to
sacrifice something in order that he may be able to
realize his fate unhindered. But more usually these
societies will be bands of consumers, of purchasers,
acting together to be more effective, combining to
finance the production of new plays or music, or to
buy pictures and statues. I do not refer to such bodies
as the National Art Collections Fund or the Friends
of the Fitzwilliam Museum. Their work is excellent.
But it only indirectly affects the living artist. No

activity of theirs would have saved Monticelli or Epstein or Van Gogh or Clare or Nerval from the hindrances and degradation of poverty. I mean rather an extension and multiplication of the Contemporary Art Society, which buys modern pictures before they have become old masters. It will be private bodies, formed in such ways, that will come to the rescue, perhaps, when the great event happens for which our prayers go up night and day, and a great writer or painter or composer appears, so monstrously blasphemous or indecent that the most hardened Municipality or University or member of the National Endowment Committee will have nothing to do with him.

There is, perhaps, one more aspect of Democracy and the Arts besides the Public and the Artist, which can be mentioned. It is one on which a whole book might throw light—two pages are useless. It is the question of what fools call the æsthetic aspirations of the community, and journalists call an atmosphere, and hard clear thinkers vow non-existent, and wise men know to be an attitude of mind. Is there anything more we can do about the artistic atmosphere in this Democracy? Is it possible to ensure that artist and critic will be living, eager about new productions and experiments, believing in their arts? What should our own attitude of mind be?

There is nothing, I suppose, to be *done*, except indirectly by smashing smugness and propriety, and encouraging enthusiasm rather than criticism in the world. All one can do is to turn out a great many artists and critics (real critics). This sort of thing is a matter of tradition largely. You get a whole lot of people, a class or a town or circle, falling naturally into the belief that Art is worth while and means a lot to them. They mostly lie. But they are necessary. Remember that, when a lot of idiots yearn to you about the Irish plays. *They* are the condition of J. M. Synge. Concerts, we hear, are hard enough to get up in Cambridge. If only those who cared for the music went they would be impossible. The Arts are built up on a crowd of prattlers, *dilettanti*, wits and pseudo-cultured. It is worth while.

But there is one thing we can do. To give vitality to the Arts it is necessary to direct a large proportion of our interest to contemporary art. The need for this is not fully recognized, especially in that half-cultivated class *we* belong to. There are two points about it I should like to mention. One is the obvious one that has already come out. It is our *duty* to be interested in contemporary art for the artist's sake, first that he may live, second that he may turn out better stuff. All your praise of Shakespeare will not turn him to his too neglected task of "blotting" at any rate *some* lines: nor will Leonardo ever complete his head of Christ. But the living, them you can stir or warm and enable to work, and work at their best. Do you think this unnecessary, slightly insulting? Is anyone muttering, "But we *are* modern and up-to-date. Nietzsche is our Bible. Van Gogh our idol. We drink in the lessons of Meredith and Ibsen and Swinburne and Tolstoy! ... Dostoieffsky and Tourgenieff. . . ." They are dead, my friends, all dead. Beware, for the generations slip imperceptibly into one another, and it is so much easier to accept standards that are prepared for you. Beware of the dead.

But it is not only a question of duty to living artists —a sufficiently dreary appeal. So much sentimentality has been talked about the immortality of Art that it is a *heresy* that I now suggest to you. To open eyes the nature of Art forbids this immortality. If you write a poem on Tuesday it begins to die on Wednesday. Some take longer dying than others. That is all. Anyhow a few thousand years will finish off the Parthenon Marbles, and Shakespeare will not outlive half a dozen more civilizations. But time has a quicker, quieter way than that. Necessary to Art is the recipient, and he must change. No man alive can read Shakespeare quite as Shakespeare meant it. The subtle shades of words have changed. The Elizabethans' common words seem strange to us. And we can never recapture the fine thrill of surprise they had at words that were delightful fresh inventions of theirs—words like *prejudice*. There is something in almost all Art that only a contemporary can get—only one who shares with the artist the general feeling for ideas and thoughts and outlook of the time. *That* is the great reason for interest in the art of one's own time. Think of what we *do* feel and value. Take—I pick almost at random—Henry James's last volume of stories, and, most delightful in the most delightful of them,[1] the phrase, "She just

[1] "A Round of Visits" in *The Finer Grain,* 1910.

charmingly hunched her eyes at him". Thirty years hence and for ever after, will they be able to get just what we get from that, in meaning and intonation, the caress of the adverb, the exact shade of comedy in the verb, the curve of the sentence?

  *   *   *   *   *

There is much to be said. But it is late, and each can say it for himself, if only he'll do what people romantically never will do, for all my persuasion— only connect Art and Democracy. Upper-class young people who live on money they don't earn and dabble with painting or writing (I am one) are always, and so finely, a little too *temperamentvoll* to be interested in "politics". It's much easier and much splendider to assume that social organization or disorganization has no effect on people—on artists at least: to fly off with some splashing war-cry that "Art will out", that "The True Artist (wonderful abstraction!) is only Improved by Poverty". The wonderful old-world romanticism of it all! The fineness, even, when it's done by poor people! It's only when it's carelessly flung out by people who *have* an assured unearned few hundreds a year, that the sentiment may ring a little discordant, taste a trifle unwholesome, something like Lord Rosebery's, to the over-sensitive palate. You feel that if the misty splendour of these artists turned perspicuous, it would for a second reveal them leaning after all against an ordinary wall, in an attitude that's exactly between the ever so slightly silly and the ever so slightly something worse. Like the lovers at the end of the modern poem:

> Flamingly, flamingly good as ends,
> Heart of my heart, are dividends.

And against them stand the politicians, who are only occupied with social and political changes: who also, less gloriously, leave Art to take care of itself. Now more than ever. "Politics", I heard two old clergymen in Oxford say, on a tram last July, "are no laughing matter nowadays". Those who never found them a laughing matter will be full these days of vaster questions than endowing artists. Their hearts thrill with great cries—Home Rule—Insurance—Peace. In such a mood "Democracy" is only a long word, a mouthful, a battle-cry, a sound that evokes tumultuous applause and right voting: or perhaps an emotional dim ideal. Regard it as a present process. The word should picture *us*, with our habits of feeling and thought, and, more particularly, thousands and millions of wakening minds everywhere. More than a million Trades Unionists, a million belonging to P.S.A. Brotherhoods, bodies with an outlook and importance we haven't dimly begun to grasp, the W.E.A., the Adult Schools—these and many more are spreading, further than ever our narrow conceits carry, fresh enthusiasms and loyalties and intellectual keenness. These, and we, and the traditions and institutions of the land, and the infinite entanglement of will and instinct and fate, individual and collective, are bound together weaving the future. It is possible and desirable to guard and aid the Arts as Democracy grows. But it must be by a conscious effort, by not being afraid of new things, by helping to build up an atmosphere and tradition of honour for the Arts, by living in the present as well as in the past, and especially, and more easily because more tangibly, by endowing artists, we can do this. Like the rest of the great adventure of Democracy it is a superb, an exhilarating chance. We, rotund and comfortable, are willy-nilly rolling out on the most amazing expedition. There's but one danger, one misconception more I would point out. Two years ago I heard a lecture on Social Reform and the Drama, delivered by a great living critic, a keen, able, solemn, whiskered, well-meaning man, Mr. William Archer. His theory was that Art depends for its subject-matter (a) on people having so much money and so much leisure as to be able to get into scrapes; (b) on social injustice and evil laws which lead to misery. Conclusion: successful social reform on democratic lines means the end of Art. He was, it is unnecessary to say, in earnest. It is a theory that has crept into too many minds. It is the ultimate disloyalty—not to Democracy, but to Art. We need not point out that all the poets and dramatists and half the painters have found their subject matter in the past. Nor need we bring up those artists from Whitman to Meunier who have begun to invade the vast new provinces now opening to them. We shall—rather we *will*—find that the old unchanging ground for the artist stands fast, the emotions of the individual human heart. Imagination will only grow profounder, passions and terrors will come in stranger shapes. Tragedy and Comedy will not leave the world while two things stay in it, the last two that Civilization will cure us of, Death and Fools. In new shapes Hamlet and Othello and Macbeth will move among us, as they do today. Though we perfect the marriage laws it will still be possible to fall in love with the wrong person or with two people; and still painful. Still, while Democracy grows, down the ages we may have the figure of a critic, an elderly man, explaining to a group of young people that the stuff of Art is being ruled out of life, black-whiskered and perplexed and in earnest—slightly resembling Matthew Arnold, a recurrent figure of most excellent comic value.